# Contents

# FOREWORD

Does your Sunday School teaching suffer from the blahs? Is your Sunday School ministry gasping for lack of fresh stimulation and new inspiration? This book is designed to broaden your perspective and give you some new ideas.

The authors of this book are two remarkable young men who have drawn upon their knowledge of God's Word and their background in Christian education, and have packaged their message in a unique style of writing that is easy to read. It is totally refreshing!

If you are like I am, you believe strongly in Sunday School education. For more than one hundred years it has effectively borne the message of Christ to millions.

I thank the Lord for the multiplied thousands of faithful Sunday School educators who have, over the decades, imparted the Bread of Life—God's Word—to generation after generation of Sunday School scholars. However, those of us who have been lifelong Sunday School attendees and patrons deserve to see a new idea now and then. The Bible's message is eternal and unchanging but the methodology can, indeed, become boring. As we look at the teaching ministry of Jesus we see a great variety in His methods of presentation. He, of course, was the Master Teacher. And I can say on the authority of God's Word that it is not sinful to regularly change your pattern of presentation. Jesus did—why shouldn't you? Have mercy on us who sit under your Sunday School ministry week after week. We love you—we believe in you—we'll always be faithful; but we are gradually turning a pale green for lack of creativity on the part of the vast majority of Sunday School educators.

The fact you are reading this book is a great source of encouragement to me. It means you are reaching out for new ideas in your teaching ministry. In my view the future of Sunday School education depends upon a continued reliance on God's Word and a strong infusion of new Bible-centered methods of Sunday School instruction. You have my enthusiasm, prayers and total optimism that you, who faithfully man the stations of Sunday School ministry every Sunday morning, will rise to the challenge of reaching forth in Christ's name to a generation of Sunday scholars who need you desperately.

Paul A. Kienel
Executive Director
Western Association of Christian Schools

# Preface

I sat in the living room of a parsonage in Pennsylvania, talking with the pastor. In a few hours I was to meet the Sunday School teachers to challenge them toward higher goals in their teaching ministries.

I had become weary of much that was traditionally associated with Christian education. There just had to be more to it than evaluating bulletin boards and giving or hearing devotionals on teaching. So much of what was called teacher training talked about everything but learning.

Perhaps, I thought, the evangelical church has earned the barb expressed in the riddle, *"When is a school not a school?"* (When it is a Sunday School!)

I shared with the pastor my burden that Sunday School teaching could be more of a valid educational experience:

1. If the Bible is related to the life-needs and experiences of the students.

2. If the students are involved in Scripture as authority.

3. If teaching is directed toward specific, measurable learning aims.

4. If the lesson is reinforced with student participation in Guided Discovery Learning.

5. If a congenial environment is developed to make learning more enjoyable.

For Sunday School teachers, either in this Pennsylvania church or elsewhere, to take these principles seriously would mean more responsibility, more accountability, and more learning.

When students are not learning, it not only means that *they* are failing to learn; it also means that the *teacher* is failing to teach!

We talked about the competition that sometimes seems insurmountable: the influences of the media—television, radio and the printed page—and the influence of secular education.

The pastor, normally a witty practical joker, became serious as he related an educational situation his seventh grade son had experienced earlier that week.

His social studies class had been discussing the morality of abortion. The teaching method that had been employed was the assignment of a role-play situation in which the seventh grade girls were to imagine that they were pregnant. They had been informed that in all likelihood the baby they were carrying would be born hopelessly deformed. The boys were to imagine they were the fathers, given the same news.

Then, based on that information, playing that role, these junior high school students were asked to make a value judgment on the rightness or wrongness of abortion.

The pastor was shocked by the subject matter. But of even more consequence was the forcefulness of the teaching method. It is hard to measure the impact that learning experiences such as these have on the thinking of young teens.

And that's one reason we are so cautious about *behavior modification* and some of the techniques applied to *values clarification*. In the classrooms of people whose values and philosophy are opposed to Christian principles, simulation, role playing, and sensitivity experimentation are often devastatingly effective methods of teaching.

As I listened to this pastor sharing his concern, I thought of our churches attempting to counteract such vivid learning experiences with lectures, often dull and frequently unrelated to the struggles of contemporary life.

I am convinced that Sunday School teaching can be more of a valid educational experience. To frustrated teachers who ask, "Can I help it if they don't learn?" I respond, "Yes! If certain principles are followed."

"But in the Septuagint text, as it has come
down to us, another paraphrase has
been interpolated into the literal translation which
Thenius would adopt as an emendation
of the Hebrew text, notwithstanding the fact
that the critical corruptness of the
Alexandrian text must be obvious to every one."

# 1
# Teach for Your Life . . . and Theirs

**Principle 1:** *Your teaching will be more effective if you relate the Bible to the life-needs and experiences of the students.*

I walked into the pastor's Sunday School class of young married adults. He had asked me to observe. It was a typical Sunday School class of young married adults. People were there with serious questions—questions about the goodness of God, perhaps. There were young mothers, with the frustrations of mastering that new role, and fathers, pinched by financial pressures. I later learned that a young couple had lost their baby earlier in the month. Were their needs going to be met?

"Class, this morning we begin our studies in the Minor Prophets."

*I wonder if the roast is burning. Or did I remember to turn the oven on?*

"Do any of you know the difference between a minor prophet and a major prophet?"

*Surely they won't really close the whole plant down, will they?*

"That's correct! Minor prophets are not at all less significant. They do have a major message."

*Will I ever be able to control Jimmy? He embarrasses me to death!*

"Now, if you turn with me in the Old Testament to the Book of Nahum, we'll discover something of the severity of God in judgment. But remember, class, even in harshness God never forgets mercy."

9

**People Are More Receptive to Life-Related Bible Teaching**
On any given Sunday morning an impartial observer could poke
his head into the average adult Sunday School class and see the
entire class gazing intently toward the teacher. A universal stare
tactic.

"You will remember, class, that last week we discussed the
third chapter of Luke."

*Oh yeah. Right!*

We can't be sure learning is happening just because eyes are
pointed in a uniform direction. The class may be polite. But when
the teacher touches life, the people tune in. That's exactly what
happened in the concluding five minutes of that Nahum class.

"I want to try to illustrate," the pastor said, "what I think
Nahum is saying to us today. A fellow pastor, a friend of mine,
was away on a business trip. A very tragic incident took place on
the day he was to return home. His wife tried to reach him by
phone in Indiana and couldn't. She tried to reach him at the air-
port in Chicago and couldn't. So she met him as he came off the
plane.

" 'Our son was killed in a car accident this afternoon.'

"He was stunned, visibly moved, but simply hung his head and
said, 'The Lord is good.'

"That's the kind of faith in God Nahum encourages us to have."

The class tuned in. But how much better it would have been to
establish that life-related principle first. It could have been
developed throughout the class session, rather than being tacked
on at the conclusion.

## Silence Is Not Necessarily Interest
It's true. Attention drifts to and from the words of a teacher
according to a great many variables. The spiritual motivation of
the listener is involved, to be sure, but so is physical fatigue.
And for that matter, so are the competing ideas that the student's
mind is attempting to sort out.

Comparative quiet and stale sameness: what an unfortunate
commentary on our educational credibility that we consistently
offer our students heavy doses of these! As we do, we grasp the

selector switch of their minds and slide them into neutral, sentencing them to another hour of restless, ethereal wandering and listless adult fantasy. We turn our classes into problem-solving sessions for the pressing concerns of the coming week of real life. While the class solves its problems in its daydreaming, we explore the ancient ruins in our teaching.

## Student Preferences Also Can Be Deceiving
"Fearfully and wonderfully made" just has to include the ability to form habits. The habits of many years may actually cause people to prefer a teacher who is easy to tune out and a classroom situation that demands little in "accountability to learning" (see chapter 3). "Sit and soak" and the third "s" is "sour," not "sanctify."

Others honestly want to learn the Bible. They attend year after yawning year. They gain perfect attendance bars until they stumble over them while ascending the church steps. But have they gained Bible knowledge? Some have. Others have not.

## There Is a Rationalization for Every Failure
There is a rationalization for every failure, and that includes failures as teachers. We may convince ourselves that something is happening. It doesn't take much. As a soft answer from an enemy turns away wrath, a nod of agreement from a student will turn away discouragement. But a nod of agreement can be quite easily solicited.

"I'm sure, students, that you can agree that the Lord has given us a tremendous blessing through this study together." (*Pause for response.*)

"You will remember from our study last week that the trumpet judgments come before the bowl judgments. Right?"

*(They'll remember. Or won't admit it if they don't.)*

## The World of Adults versus the Real World of Children
Children are a different breed. They throw things, kick their neighbors, and make strange noises. Why? They're intent on informing their teachers when they fail to hold their attention. And

children are woefully faithful in sending those little bliss-busting messages.

It is helpful to recognize these messages as indications that learning is not happening. But when children are involved in the learning process, and the Bible is taught life-relatedly (even on *their* level of understanding), they tune in.

### Meanwhile Back at Nahum

The same kind of shift happened in the Nahum adult Sunday School class. The shuffle from Old Testament to contemporary life was a real rouser. The jolt came when the teacher touched his students at a point they could readily identify with. Most of us will not be attacked by a hoard of Assyrians, but death is all too real. Is it any wonder they tuned in?

### Youth: Turned On and Tuned In. How?

There is still a segment of the evangelical church with a caste system that brands youth unreachable. These people maintain that we can give them parties; bring on the pizza; perhaps a youth choir will "go"; or basketball, volleyball, tennis, beach parties and badminton. But learning?

"Youth will not listen to lectures."

"You may be able to convert them. But you can't teach them."

Unreachable. Unteachable. Really?

Youth are eager for meaningful involvement in learning, not just token participation. But it must touch life; when it does they tune in. When the connection with life is remote, they turn off and tune out, unless they are already unusually motivated.

### Attention Span and Pilot Lights

A Sunday School class is like a battery of television cameras. In producing a live telecast many cameras are pointed toward the action, but only the one with the illuminated red pilot light is sending a signal through the control board.

Students—children, youth, or adults—may be pointed toward the teacher, but that doesn't mean the message is being received and channeled to their learning apparatus.

In the process of teaching we are constantly losing and gaining the attention of our audience. And in the process, the high point of our life-relatedness will generally correspond to the high point of audience attention.

Speaking of attention, commercial advertising men are out to get ours. They live in a world of competition which is hard on them, but it's not easy on us either.

It has been estimated, by people who estimate such things, that the average U.S. adult, in a given day, is exposed to 500 commercial advertising messages. That same average adult watches 44 hours of television a week (which averages out to six and one-half hours a day) and spends 32 minutes a day reading a newspaper or magazine. This kind of input has its influence!

It has forced us to fabricate an elaborate system of filters to keep irrelevant debris out of our thinking process. Research seems to indicate that the average adult is rather successful with his filters. He manages to block out 85 percent of those commercial messages so that he consciously perceives only 75 of them. He is unaware that he was exposed to the other 425 and he only *acts* on two and one-half percent of the 500 he was initially exposed to (see diagram 1).

Since people responding to ads is Madison Avenue's bread and butter, to say nothing of its steak and lobster, one would naturally expect a certain level of expertise to surface in the advertising business. And it has: the sharpest, most exhilarating, colorful, vibrant, professionally-executed, life-related, top quality job. There's not a great deal that they spare in grabbing our attention.

Ad men, it should be clear to the consumer, pursue the average U.S. adult. They stalk him, identifying his felt needs, experiences, and interests. They exploit every possible hook to snag his drifting, filtered interest.

In the process, the subject matter of the commercial may have little to do with the intrinsic worth of the product, but the consumer hears and responds, consciously or unconsciously, to that which captures his interest.

We must not borrow their manipulative methodology nor duplicate their deceitfulness. But successful communication—and

**DIAGRAM 1**

teaching *is* communication—must take account of that elaborate filtering process.

The media-saturated minds of our contemporaries experience increasing difficulty turning on to lecture situations. We contribute to that difficulty when our teaching has little or no relevance to life.

The biblical communicator with scriptural answers for the frustrations and spiritual conflicts of the average student can open the channels for Bible learning. The frazzled disillusionment of the 20th century can provide the impetus for responsive communication and its by-product, learning.

But when teachers fail to appeal to the life-needs and experiences of their students, the filters are activated and the Bible knowledge so desperately needed is sifted onto the floor of the church's educational complex.

## Motivation: Pressure Cooker or Crock Pot?

College, graduate school, seminary; these are pressure-cooker learning environments while Sunday School could be compared to a crock pot. Each has its level of motivation.

The problem is that most of us teach others in the way we were taught. Where did we get our model? What kind of learning situations were we subjected to? For the most part, the pressure cooker.

Three motivational factors were given high visibility: (1) the possibility of *rewards*, (2) the prospect of *punishment*, (3) the reality of *rivalry*. Every time we were tempted to get out of line we were confronted with one of the three: a gradebook, a disciplinary measure, or a classmate's scholarship (see diagram 2). This was our teaching model.

So after an elementary education, a junior and senior high school education, and perhaps college and graduate school, the potential Sunday School teacher walks out of those hallowed halls into the Sunday School annex, up to the lectern, and teaches as though he could grade, punish, and graduate students *cum laude*.

Learning tends to rise or fall to meet the level of motivation. What are we appealing to?

If a person learns *solely* for the grade, what happens to his learning when the gradebook is burned? Or when the threat of punishment is removed? Or after all the honors have been bestowed and the remaining vestiges are a diploma, and a few crumpled snapshots?

Rewards, punishment, and rivalry are *perhaps* indispensable ingredients in the pressure cooker, but Sunday School is a crock pot.

Sunday School classes should simmer in Scripture's knowledge

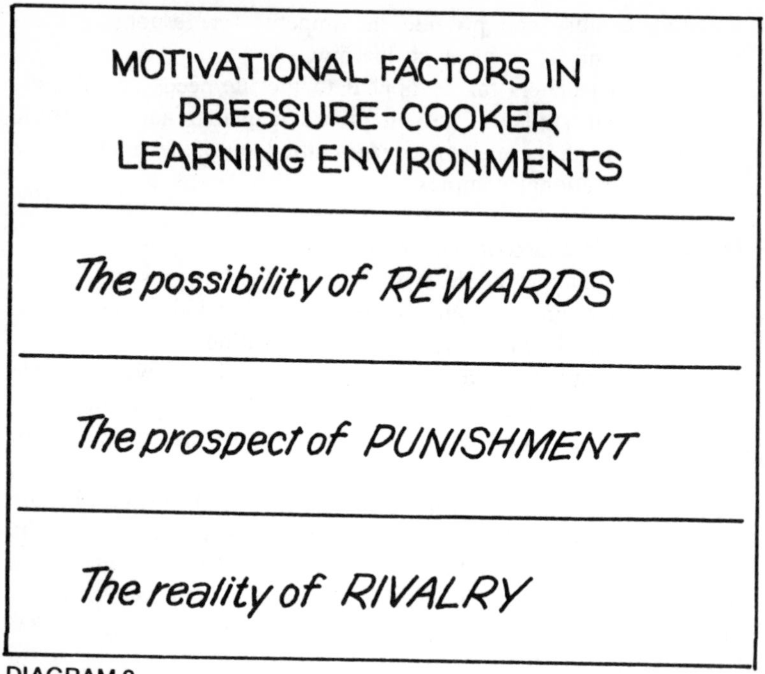

---

### MOTIVATIONAL FACTORS IN PRESSURE-COOKER LEARNING ENVIRONMENTS

---

*The possibility of* REWARDS

---

*The prospect of* PUNISHMENT

---

*The reality of* RIVALRY

---

DIAGRAM 2

for life. That's the motivational factor we should be appealing to. The Bible is more than *academia*. It is a life-related textbook and must be taught that way.

So we begin with the *felt needs* of the class and orient our presentation to those needs. The product will be learning motivated by life and its struggles, not artificial factors such as a gradebook that can be removed.

A felt need is not that hard to identify. It is a *problem to be solved;* something that is a problem to the students. It can also be a point of *curiosity to satisfy*. The class may not be curious about the same things as theologians. Perhaps there are *frustrations to relieve*. Or information that is properly identified as *knowledge needed for life*.

All of Scripture, properly presented, fits this model (see diagram 3).

### Am I an Editor or a Communicator?

We do not determine what is relevant or irrelevant in Scripture. We are not *editors* of the Bible, but we are *communicators*. As communicators we have a responsibility to approach our teaching time with the question: "How can I help make learning happen?"

An honest and enlightened inquiry will doubtless lead us to teach with extreme concern for the life-needs and experiences of our students. People are more receptive to life-related Bible teaching.

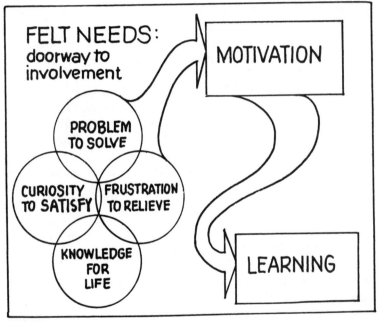

DIAGRAM 3

**Practice While You Teach—1**

Concept: *People are more receptive to life-related Bible teaching.* Use these points to evaluate the life-relatedness of your Bible teaching.

1. I am the only one who talks during the Sunday School class session (check one):

always     usually     sometimes     seldom     never

2. *How do you respond to this statement? Why?*
"Problems with discipline or boredom always indicate a failure to involve the students in learning, and a failure to teach life-relatedly."
*agree strongly     agree     disagree     disagree strongly*

3. I approach my task as a Sunday School teacher as if I had the authority to grade my students (check one):
*always     usually     sometimes     seldom     never*

4. The following difficulties are typical of the problems and frustrations my students face during a typical month . . . *(Complete the sentence.)*

5. When it comes to Bible knowledge, my students seem to have a curiosity about . . . *(Complete the sentence.)*

To be fully equipped with God's answers for my students' lives, they need to know about such things as . . . *(Complete the sentence.)*

## People Need Life-Related Bible Teaching

The pastor of a small church in the Midwest shook his head and with a slight, uncomprehending smile, spilled his frustration.

"I just can't understand this Bill Gothard thing. From what I can tell he isn't sharing anything new that I haven't been teaching my people for years. And it's a struggle to get them out to church. But Gothard has a seminar and they drive hundreds of miles to hear him."

Defensiveness. This pastor is not a solo voice on the critical score for Gothard and his nationally known seminars. There are other evangelical leaders singing the same tune.

Having plucked Gothard's doctrinal feathers, some of the critics insistently, if not proudly, affirm that their own theological purity soars to greater heights.

But the seminar has taken off and its success is a forceful reminder that people recognize the need of Bible knowledge that touches very specifically and directly on areas of conflicts and values in Christian living. Consequently, the seminar has sensitized the evangelical church to the desperately needed priority of relating Bible knowledge to specific life-needs. If that were its *only* contribution, it would be praiseworthy.

The factory worker has questions, temptations, and areas of compromise all around him. They need to be faced.

The young housewife has her own set of daily frustrations. Her problems are compounded by the confused values and continual bombardment of humanistic and anti-Christian media.

Many parents admit heartbroken failure, failure that now seems irreversible in the lives of their children.

### Content for Content's Sake

Content for content's sake *may* be a necessary part of the discipline of higher education, but it is a poor substitute for what should be happening in our Sunday School classes.

And what should be happening? A compassionate and loving ministry of the Word of God, applied to the life-needs and experiences of the students. If the intensity of their needs is beyond the teacher's comprehension, those students will probably carry out of class the same problems they carried in. Weekly.

On the other hand, if their real world of kinks and tangled questions has a place in the teacher's understanding, he'll never again feel comfortable mediating content for content's sake.

### Jesus, for Example

Jesus' experience of temptation in the wilderness has long been recognized and often cited as proof that Scripture is our resource to withstand temptation. But Scripture must be specifically applied, not vaguely tossed at a given situation, which presupposes a tremendous reservoir of Bible knowledge, integrated with the life-needs and experiences of the student.

Jesus is the Son of God. He was able to draw upon divine wisdom in a unique way. But He carefully applied objective Bible knowledge in countering each of Satan's temptations.

Our Sunday Schools are populated with students who have been exposed to hours of church-oriented educational experiences but have never learned to relate the facts of the Bible to their life-experiences. It seems a fundamental principle has been missed.

### Grocery-list Teaching Doesn't Bring Home the Bacon

Reciting all the facts on any topic—carefully arranged religious minutiae—is not effective teaching. Conscientiously applied, a curriculum that has been used in a Sunday School for years may be applicable to needs. But reciting truths like items on a grocery list generally falls short of meeting people's needs in the market-place of life.

Bill Gothard has stood before thousands at a given seminar with, of necessity, broad basic assumptions and generalities regarding the needs and conflicts of his audience. But he has hit them with an amazing level of God-given insight.

And yet, the Sunday School teacher has the opportunity to know all his students in a more personal way. The teacher could use his hour for life-changing, two-way communication. And it's the teacher who often fails to get below surface, cursory, vague application when he is merely presenting a grocery list of religious facts.

### Five Minutes: Last Chance for Life

There is a basic flaw in our traditional approach to Sunday School teaching: The Fatal Five Minute Application Tack-On.

As was the case with our Nahum Sunday School illustration, traditional Sunday School teaching has often reserved the final fleeting moments of class time for the application or lesson for life.

But by the time the teacher gets around to relating factual content to life-needs and experiences, much of the time period is lost. All too often the students' interest is lost as well.

If we spend too much of our exposition in the ancient ruins of the Holy Land, we might not make it back to contemporary reality in time to give a parting principle for life. And if the specific need or problem is not brought into focus *before* the content is presented, it should not be surprising if the class misses the life application that may subsequently be developed.

### The Spiritual Submarine Sandwich

In an attempt to break away from the last-minute *Salvage a Lesson for Life Syndrome*, some well-intentioned teachers have developed a *content/life dichotomy* by opening class with an *application-approach* and, after the meat of the Word, closing the lesson with an *application-conclusion*. Sort of a spiritual submarine sandwich: the meat of the Word between two indirectly related slices of application.

Factual religious truth is neither freestanding without application, nor is it to be served as a "here's the knowledge/here's the application" sandwich. It is a unity. A whole. God's Word is itself life-related.

### Where's the Holy Spirit in All This?

Perhaps we have all sensed times when the Holy Spirit has used our poorly-prepared, feeble teaching efforts and has accomplished astonishing things with them. Pastors often joke of receiving the most fragrant accolades on some of their most poorly-prepared sermons.

But we should not plan on it. The ministry of the Holy Spirit is not a cop-out for sterile efforts at application to life.

### What Do I Do with My Curriculum?

Even instructional materials that follow the "here's the knowledge/ here's the application" format can be effective if we focus on the present conflicts and spiritual needs of the students. Teachers who do this soon learn that the hassles of their students are not unlike their own hassles.

When the Word of God is prayerfully and compassionately presented for what it is, an intensely practical and relevant guide for real people who face real hassles, life-changing learning often takes place. People *need* life-related Bible teaching.

### Practice While You Teach—2

Concept: *People need life-related Bible teaching.*
Use these points to evaluate the life-relatedness of your Bible teaching.

1. At times when I have taught material to my class that has touched very specifically and directly on areas of values and conflicts in Christian living, my class has . . . *(Complete the sentence.)*

2. The Bible becomes a resource to combat temptation, for me and my students, when . . . *(Complete the sentence.)*

3. *How do you respond to this statement? Why?*

"Most students, though exposed to hours and hours of church-oriented Bible education, are unable to relate the Bible to their life-needs and experiences."

*agree strongly     agree     disagree     disagree strongly*

4. Without exposing specific sins or embarrassing people, I could help my students deal with their deepest inner problems if I . . . *(Complete the sentence.)*

5. I carefully identify the life-related point of each lesson I teach, weaving it throughout the entire class presentation.

*always     usually     sometimes     seldom     never*

## The Bible Itself Is the Pattern
## for Life-Related Bible Teaching

The teacher had obviously spent an enormous amount of time preparing but somehow it just fell flat. He *seemed* to know his subject rather well, in fact, but to tell the *truth,* he was just reading.

"The archaeological evidence from Tell es-Sultan is not clear regarding the destruction. The excavations conducted at the site back in 1930 and 1936 indicate that the city was occupied down to the year 1550 B.C. Probably by the Hyksos peoples . . . and then in the late Bronze Age . . ."

The class started out interesting, but became harder to swallow as the students began to choke on the dust.

The class session continued, and at length concluded with scarcely a mention of anything *religious,* let alone Christian. It would have been proper in the Near Eastern history department of a secular college; or perhaps at a special lecture at the neighborhood synagogue; or a seminary class on historical backgrounds of the Old Testament. But in Sunday School it was poor, an inappropriate use of good material. There was virtually no awareness of the class, no cognizance of their life-needs.

## Bible Knowledge and Behavior Change

Scripture is intended to touch life and bear the fruit of *behavior change.* Bible knowledge as mere factual content should not be considered as an end in itself. Scripture constantly identifies specific areas of sinful behavior, attitudes, and frustrations as the backdrop for the giving of God's revelation.

The Apostle Paul's Spirit-inspired writings, for example, are identified as directly relating to the needs of specific individuals and groups. Paul wrote the Book of Romans to fulfill a specific need for the Christians at Rome, pending the opportunity to personally visit the church to "impart some spiritual gift . . . [that they] may be established" (Rom. 1:11). It is a unique blend of doctrine and life.

In First and Second Corinthians, Paul talked about such things as carnal divisions, immorality, lawsuits, marriage, and sexual problems.

Galatians, a doctrinal high-water mark in the New Testament, squares away misconceptions about what it means to be religious. In the process the Apostle deals with sensuality, factions, outbursts of anger, how to please God, love, joy, peace, and his well-known appeal to carry one another's burdens.

In the Book of Philippians Paul discussed "The Kenosis of Christ"—what Christ surrendered to be totally identified with man. It is given as an illustration of the attitudes we should have toward one another.

The Thessalonian Epistles present the end times in today's setting. Christians are admonished not to grieve despairingly over dead Christians, to encourage the fainthearted, to help the weak, work if they want to eat, and more.

Each book is profitable for our rebuke, restoration, and ongoing training in righteous living.

Suffering, pain, hardships, joy, love, marriage, divorce, anxiety, contentment, and thought-life. This is stuff the New Testament is made of. Not disjointed "last-thought/by-the-way application." Life is inseparably locked into the movement of thought and argument of the Old and New Testament books.

## Why Isn't It Taught That Way?

When our goal is learning the Word of God we sometimes justifiably deal in exhaustive detail. The writer's point may tend to get muddled in our exploration: verse-by-verse, phrase-by-phrase, even breath-by-breath. It's *almost* excusable that we would miss the forest while we inspect the bark, pine needles, and sap.

For all that is gained in detailed, in-depth Bible study, however, far too often we do sacrifice our understanding of broad principles. Sometimes we miss the very principles that the writer was trying to communicate to his readers with those jots and tittles we so scrutinously dissect, studying in depth.

That's poor technique and may account for our propensity to isolate doctrine and duty. We have studied them independently for so long we've forgotten that the original hearers got the whole message of a given book at once (with the obvious exception of some of the Old Testament books). They might have missed an aorist here or an ablative there, but they would not have missed the principles.

It has long been the Protestant tradition that doctrine must be preached practically, and duties doctrinally.

As we ponder the prospects of teaching systematic theology to our life-hungry Sunday School classes, we might remember that systematic theology is the result of laborious, painful study aimed at distilling the theological substance out of its life-related context.

There may be a place for that. But we must realize what we're doing and consider the needs of the class.

### Remember the Pharisees?

Unapplied Bible knowledge is dangerous stuff. It makes people more hardened in sin or at least less responsive to the "still, small voice" accompanies the ministration of God's Word.

Let's remember the Pharisees! They were experts in the Old Testament, but while straining at gnats, they bounced into a regular camel-swallowing act.

There is the ever-present peril of turning people into their own brand of contemporary camel-swallowing Pharisee, proud of religious knowledge, but devoid of piercing life application.

### Word of God: Prophets and Profit

The Bible has a great deal to say about itself, and much of what it says deals with the concept of life-relatedness:

- It is food for the soul (Deut. 8:3).
- Its precepts are to be written on the heart (Deut. 6:6).
- It furnishes light (Ps. 19:8).
- It is powerful in its influence (Rom. 1:16).
- It is a spiritual defense (Eph. 6:17).
- It discerns thoughts and intentions (Heb. 4:12).
- It is a purifier of life (Ps. 119:9).
- It was written for a life-changing purpose (John 20:31; 1 Cor. 10:11; 1 John 5:13).
- It is profitable for instruction (Deut 4:10; 2 Tim 3:16–17).
- God's approval is linked with a proper grasp of His Word (2 Tim. 2:15).

This is not an exhaustive list. The great passages of the Bible that are commonly used to support scriptural instruction as a priority of the Church are all directly oriented toward changing life-values and behavior patterns.

## WORD OF GOD: PROPHETS AND PROFIT
### 2 Timothy 3:16

| TERM: | EXPLANATION: | APPLICATION: |
|---|---|---|
| DOCTRINE | TEACHING | Imparting God's principles and truth |
| REPROOF | CONVICTION | Application to particular relationships and needs |
| CORRECTION | RESTORATION | Steps of action toward uprightness |
| INSTRUCTION | TRAINING | Ongoing guidance—discipline, understanding, direction |

DIAGRAM 4

Probably the most incisive statement of the instructive purposes of the Word of God is found in 2 Timothy 3:16–17, verses commonly quoted when discussing the doctrine of the Bible. "All Scripture is given by inspiration of God and is profitable for doctrine, for reproof, for correction, for instruction in righteousness: that the man of God may be perfect, thoroughly furnished unto all good works" (KJV).

That is intensely practical.

Scripture not only imparts God's principles in the form of factual data; it also shows us areas where our style of life deviates from Scripture's dictates. It restores us to uprightness as we submissively respond to the Spirit's ministry of the Word in our lives. It continues the process in an ongoing ministry of discipline (see diagram 4).

Verse 17 begins with a word indicating *purpose*. God gave us an infallible, divinely inspired, life-related Book in order that we might be adequate and equipped. Equipped for life and for every good work.

### Where Do I Begin?

Teaching the Bible life-relatedly requires balancing four essential elements (see diagram 5, page 27).

*A Proper Biblical Interpretation* Sound application of Scripture to life-needs must begin with a clear, proper biblical interpretation. If the interpretation of what the Bible *means* is wrong, the lesson is hardly salvaged with a life application. There must be an understanding of the implications of Scripture in its historical/ grammatical/cultural setting before we can accurately transfer it into our contemporary cultural context.

This does not necessitate our sharing everything we know about history, grammar, and culture every time we teach!

*A Principle-Oriented Approach* Skillful application of the Bible to life observes the life principles presented in Scripture. If we become bogged down in interpretive exercises and excessive details of exegesis and exposition, we may fail to discern broad movements of thought and their implications for life.

Example: In writing to the Corinthians, Paul talked about

some of Israel's post-exodus experiences. "Now these things happened as examples for us, that we should not crave evil things, as they also craved" (1 Cor. 10:6). That *principle* from an Old Testament experience is subsequently developed in this chapter of 1 Corinthians. Examination of detail alone often misses such principles.

*A Contemporary Outlook* Lessons that touch lives are lessons which succeed in bringing the learners out of the dusty roads of Palestine into the asphalt of today. At the same time they are lessons which carry knowledge gained and principles gleaned from that educational field trip to yesterday.

The Bible must be related to our contemporary hassles and experiences. Principles, based on a sound biblical interpretation, must be transmitted into our cultural setting.

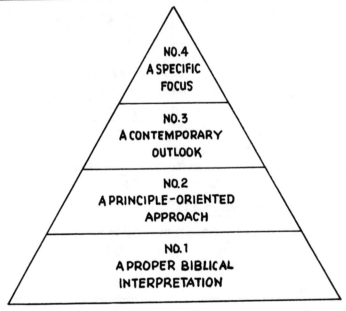

**BUILDING LIFE-RELATED TEACHING**

DIAGRAM 5

*A Specific Focus* Applications such as, "This shows us that we should study the Bible more" or "We need to really trust the Lord" are inadequate. Scripture is more piercing, more direct. It deals with our lives and interpersonal relationships in forceful, pinching specifics. Our applications should do the same (see diagram 6).

---

# IS MY TEACHING LIFE-RELATED ?

---

### 1. *A PROPER BIBLICAL INTERPRETATION*

Does the life application rise out of a proper biblical interpretation ?
*Have I clarified what the passage means ?*

### 2. *A PRINCIPLE-ORIENTED APPROACH*

Does the life application relate a principle for life ?
*Am I getting bogged down giving detail and theory without touching life ?*

### 3. *A CONTEMPORARY OUTLOOK*

Does the life application bring the lesson to today's reality ?
*Have I gone beyond the historical situation to the contemporary setting ?*

### 4. *A SPECIFIC FOCUS*

Does the life application lead to a specific confrontation with life ?
*Is it vague and general ?*

---

DIAGRAM 6

**What About the Stuff That Just Doesn't Seem Practical?**
The content of Bible history, outlines of Bible chronology, and

outlines to analyze chapter or book content all qualify as legitimate for doctrinal teaching. It is important to see, however, that Paul (2 Tim. 3:16–17) did not teach that *all* Scripture is profitable for *doctrine*, with *a few selected passage* profitable for correction or *training in righteousness.*

Therefore, when planning content for an instructional period of an hour or less per week, we should think *life-relatedly.* Lengthy passages that are strong in historical and/or geographical teaching should be covered in less detail. They should be dealt with at a level of detail that would allow every unit of Sunday School instruction to be life-related, principle-oriented, and relevant for conviction, restoration, and training.

Those who are more mature can appropriately probe deeper into areas of historical, grammatical, geographical, and archaeological insight.

### Milk, Meat, and Maturity

Paul told the Corinthians, "I gave you milk to drink, not solid food; for you were not yet able to receive it" (1 Cor. 3:2).

If a similar situation existed in some of our churches, we would still be trying to cram a steak down those drooling spiritual infants. And they'd probably still be infants.

We must not condone immaturity, but must admit that infants *choke on meat* and *grow on milk.*

All Scripture is appropriate for use in Sunday School. But the level of depth at which the content is probed must take into consideration the level of spiritual maturity of the class members. Their abilities to receive conviction, restoration, and training from each unit of Bible study must be evaluated and considered a determining factor in our style of teaching.

The Bible itself is the pattern for life-related Bible teaching.

### Practice While You Teach—3

Concept: *The Bible itself is the pattern for life-related Bible teaching.* Use these points to evaluate the life-relatedness of your Bible teaching.

1. *How do you respond to this statement? Why?*

"Since the Word was originally given against the backdrop of specific ideas of sinful behavior, or at least, life-related values, it is never proper to teach it with a merely academic approach.''

agree strongly     agree     disagree     disagree strongly

2. When teaching a passage in great detail, I keep the basic life-principle of that passage before my mind, and the minds of my students by . . . (Complete the sentence.)

3. "Doctrine must be preached practically, and duties doctrinally." If I am to be consistent with this principle, when I teach material that is more heavily doctrinal I will keep it practical by . . . (Complete the sentence.)

When I am teaching material that is overtly practical, I will make the doctrinal foundation clear by . . . (Complete the sentence.)

4. In my teaching ministry, I am careful to see that my class clearly understands the interpretation of the Scripture, not just my ideas of application.

always     usually     sometimes     seldom     never

5. For the purposes of Sunday School teaching, I am careful to see that the material I teach is covered at a level of depth that still allows each class session to be life-related.

always     usually     sometimes     seldom     never

"There are plenty of verses I could use today,
but I won't take the time to do that!
I just want you to know that this backsliding
into worldly patterns of dress and music has
just got to stop!
Now! Now! Now! Now! Now!"

# 2

# Give 'em the Word . . .
# Not Just Your Word

**Principle 2:** *Your teaching will be more effective if you involve the students in Scripture as the authority.*

Lynda flopped down in the tan folding chair and slid her paperbound New Testament across the table. She brushed her scraggly, strawberry blond hair away from the corners of her mouth, giggling nervously. Repositioning her gum, she wrinkled her brow in concentration.

We were at a seminar with a prominent Christian educator. As a part of a research situation, 25 young people from evangelical churches in the Phoenix, Arizona area were brought together to meet with about the same number of youth workers and Christian educators.

The question: "How does your church use the Bible to help you solve your problems?"

Lynda responded this way:

"Lynda, you go to a good Bible-teaching church, right?"

"Yeah."

"The people at your church use the Bible a lot, do they?"

"Sure."

"We're trying to zero in on the concept that those of us who have the Bible really have a tremendous advantage over the people who don't have the Bible. Do you agree with that concept?"

"Of course."

"Well, Lynda, you mentioned earlier that one problem you face is a lack of confidence in yourself. You said you were a bit worried about the future, not knowing for sure what's coming and whether you can handle it."

"Yes, but I do think the Lord has the answers and stuff."

"OK, great! Lynda, you said you have been shown answers from the Word of God. Can you explain *how* the Bible was the answer to you? How was it used?"

She paused, thoughtfully considering the question. The chair creaked as she shifted. She looked puzzled and pensive.

How *was* the Bible used?

How did it give answers?

"Well, at our church we have the greatest people. I mean like, well, our teacher is really a neat guy. When I had a problem about what to do with my life, I mean he said I don't need to worry about my future, or feel out of it and stuff 'cause I got the Word of God."

She went on, "They're always telling us that we really need God's Word . . . we really ought to study it and read it."

## Typical Christian Teenagers
Question: What could be more interesting than an interview with a typical Christian teenager? Answer: The tabulated results of 25 interviews with typical Christian teenagers!

Only 2 out of the 25 described situations in which they were actively involved in finding answers in the Bible for themselves. The others described situations in which "concerned adult leaders" told them what the Bible's answers were.

And it seems this phenomenon is not unique to youth work. When it comes to the Bible and learning in evangelical churches, children and adults as well as youth find it quite difficult, if not impossible, to eke out, unassisted, biblical answers for their tangled problems.

The wall-to-wall majority of us find ourselves taking one or two of the following three approaches to our teaching.

### The Bible as a Club Approach
The Word is a sword, to be sure, but it is the Spirit's sword, not a club in the teacher's hand. Far too often the situation degen-

erates and the Spirit's sword becomes our club. And that's not good.

The following yarn could be spun on this point.

The representative teacher approaches the lectern. He glances at the clock on the wall, then down at his wristwatch. The class is late, except for one timid high school sophomore boy and three nice girls. The teacher nods a congenial "hello" to these faithful four and then heads for the crowded hallway.

After repeated attempts to obtain a quorum, the class begins. The teacher prays that there will be more faithful high schoolers "to stand in the gap."

The text for the morning is 1 John 2:15, "Love not the world" (KJV). He reads it and closes his Bible. The next 20 minutes are consumed with the teacher's valid complaints about loose moral standards among high school kids these days. He cites freaky clothes, loud music, and unbiblical haircuts as choice examples of worldliness, while waving and pounding his Bible. The Bible has high visibility, but is this really Bible teaching?

Boys slouched in the back roll their eyeballs. A few girls giggle. The teens who are already faithful feel a renewed sense of concern over the church youth group. The superintendent nervously pokes his head in the door three times, trying to hint, without siding with the rowdies, that it *is* time to close.

What went wrong? Bad ideas? Poor content? Inappropriate topic? Not necessarily. The approach is wrong.

In this situation a teacher's ideas become the priority. Everything begins here. The Bible becomes, at best, a filter for his thoughts. At worst, it is a club for clobbering sinning students. In his zeal to apply the Word to others, a teacher may effectively insulate himself from its obvious demands on his own life-style.

## One Crucial Question

Here's the crucial question: "When a teacher has completed his task, does a student feel accountable to the Bible, or merely to a teacher?"

When a teacher approaches his class "armed with his Bible," gunning for his students, ready to share his ideas and "back 'em

# Approach No. 1
## "THE BIBLE-AS-A-CLUB APPROACH"

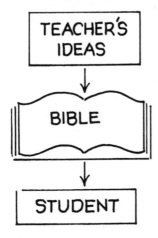

DIAGRAM 7

up with Bible," he may succeed and fail simultaneously. He may succeed at instilling guilt, but fail at producing maturity. He may succeed at sharing his own ideas, but fail to lead the class to the Bible and *its* viewpoint.

To whom does a teacher make a student feel accountable? *There's* the crucial question.

Does a student feel "I must change to agree with the teacher"?

Or, "I must change because it is what God expects"?

### Word of God: Text or Proof Text?

Most of us who are involved in Bible-teaching churches are taught good ideas. And our teachers often know the Bible rather well. Available curriculum materials are rich resources to equip a teacher with good ideas and acceptable methods.

But the prime point, and (lamentably) the point of common failure, is *how* the Bible is *used*. Is it called on to reinforce a teacher's good ideas? Or is a student led into the Word to discover

God's authoritative truth? Is the Bible the text of study, or merely the proof text to juice up a teacher's arguments?

Proof-text teaching comes more easily than involving a student, but the results are often disheartening.

## Stone-Instead-of-Bread Teaching

As the evangelical church, we are precariously close to bringing up a generation of kids who have only known the value system of the older generation.

"You want the Word of God to guide your life? Then don't dress like that" or, "listen to this music" or a host of other legalistic requirements. Most of them are good. Many are derived from Scripture itself. But when we substitute *our good advice* for the authority of the Bible, we give a stone instead of bread, a serpent instead of fish.

Will the students be prepared to meet only the temptations that the teacher specifically preaches against? Or will they be equipped with biblical principles and the capacity to uncover biblical answers on their own?

What will happen when the next year introduces some new-fangled thing, some fresh breed of sin? Will those students be equipped to handle it without "a concerned adult leader" there to prop them up?

I remember when we used to spend half our time convincing kids that dancing and movies were sinful. Somehow it seemed so much simpler then, before so many kids on campus were blowing their minds on the drug scene; before the "free love, loose morals" surge.

Students will come home with new-fangled games the old folks never played. They can leave home prepared if they are taught the principle of personal submission to the Bible as authority, rather than given a list of taboos.

## Seed, Soil, Sword, Club

The seed of the Word will have great difficulty germinating in the life soil of a disciple who has never learned this principle of submission. The maturing process has been interrupted. The uprooted remains of what might have been a powerful disciple is the wilting testimony of unclaimed potential.

When the Sword of the Spirit becomes the club of a teacher, the result is recorded in bruised disciples.

It is one thing to be able to nail a floundering Follower of the Way with a battery of pertinent verses. It is quite another matter to patiently guide a student in his own investigation of the Word of God. The first may produce gasping discipleship which dies when the influence of a teacher is removed. The second will provide the life-giving nutriment of personal accountability to God's Word. God uses a sharp, double-edged sword, not our blunt opinions.

## Practice While You Teach—4

Concept:  *The Bible-as-a-Club Approach may produce bruised disciples.* Use these points to evaluate your approach to teaching.

1. My class could get *almost* as much out of my teaching if they did not bring their Bible, but *did* listen very attentively.
*always     usually     sometimes     seldom     never*

2. If I asked my class to list what I am *for* and what I am *against*, their longest list would be . . . *(Complete the sentence.)*

3. When I begin preparing my lesson, I begin by evaluating how obedient I am to the principles I am going to teach.
*always     usually     sometimes     seldom     never*

4. I help my class to understand the difference between my opinions and what the Bible teaches by . . . *(Complete the sentence.)*

5. My class would be better prepared to handle problems in the future if I . . . *(Complete the sentence.)*

### The Chair-of-Theology Approach

Lynda and the other seminar participants described three teaching approaches they had experienced in their fundamental churches. Predictably, lamentably, the Bible-as-a-Club Approach predominated.

But a second approach was also noted, namely, the Chair-of-Theology Approach. We might diagram it like this:

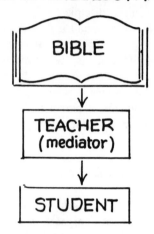

## Approach No. 2
## "THE CHAIR-OF-THEOLOGY APPROACH"

**DIAGRAM 8**

Here the teacher becomes the Bible authority. It differs from the first approach in that there is more use of the Bible. The teacher derives great satisfaction from his role as interpreter, explainer, "apply-er." But in the process, the student's direct involvement in the Word is short-circuited.

So the representative teacher begins by selecting a text, or having one selected for him. Where he goes from there is important. *How* he goes from there is enlightening.

Some of our typical teens expressed it like this:

"The Bible is the answer because, well, like we were going through 1 Corinthians in our Sunday School class. And the teacher showed us how it said this neat stuff about love."

Or, "When we were in 1 John, our teacher told us about not loving the world. He told us that was our problem if we spent a lot of money on clothes and records and stuff."

### Mediators and Mini-Popes

Note the teacher's prominence in this process. There is more use of the Word, but it is through the teacher acting as mediator.

Now, here we trim a hairline point, but there *is* an important distinction to be observed. Teacher and student have not come together on common ground before the Word. A student is considered a learner, but the teacher sees himself as an authority, a mediator of truth, a professor on the chair of theology.

This leads a student to feel accountable to his teacher more than, and sometimes instead of, the Word.

Some teachers become so taken up with their position they begin to view themselves as mini-popes, opening doors of understanding with Kingdom Keys or combinations which only *they* know.

Few teachers *mean* to do this, but many succeed at it, with unnerving accuracy.

The difficulty here is not so much with the words that are spoken. It is an *attitudinal* problem, usually subconscious, but nevertheless quite real.

We may be transmitting Bible. At the same time they may be receiving messages like, "You really need me. You cannot understand the Bible without me. I am a scholar."

Here's a test: If a class is awestruck over our scholarship and ability we may be failing. We need to check our transmitters and their receivers.

We are all easily swayed by the compliments of those who stand in awe of our ability. But there is often a sad corollary: the more we may impress a class, the more confident they may become that they can never understand and apply the Bible for themselves.

## Coffee and Koinonia

Some of the richest koinonia-type fellowship is brewed without beans. Yet it isn't "instant." It takes time to perk up personal relationships, but it's well worth the effort.

The teacher who slides into a cold classroom just in time to share the stuff often falls most naturally into approach number two. It is easy to feel like a guest lecturer, a visiting authority, in your own church.

On the other hand, the warmer the personal relationships with students, the harder it is to play the Chair-of-Theology role.

Koinonia fellowship, with or without the coffee, can work wonders in the weekly grind. When you share together as caring co-members of the Body of Christ, it is only natural to stand before the Word on common ground.

## What about Pulpits and Pews?

At first, or even second glance, the diagram of the second approach may resemble church—Bible, Teacher-mediator, and Students. It appears that the second approach reflects the accepted concept of pulpit ministry. Perhaps that's why our Sunday School classes often look like replicas of adult church, the JV, of which church is varsity.

But just what is varsity?

The most Spirit-filled and effective New Testament preachers did not need pulpits to pound home their point. It was modeled in their consistent style of life.

Yes, they had authority.

True, they often introduced new revelation from God.

Granted, they did not "pool ignorance" in undirected, ill-prepared discussion sessions.

But their selling point was a changed life. To insist on a place of authority, yet not model the truth taught, is a bad advertisement for the church.

Pulpits and pews? Sure, but not at the expense of personal relationships! Paul almost apologized for pleading his authority (2 Cor. 11:1).

"We," Paul said, "proved to be gentle among you, as a nursing mother tenderly cares for her own children. Having thus a fond affection for you, we were well pleased to impart to you not only the gospel but also our own lives, because you had become very dear to us" (1 Thes. 2:7–8).

A man can *dogmatically mediate* truth to others. Or he can stand in personal humility and spiritual influence, leading others to follow his submission to the Word. Any congregation can accurately sense the difference, regardless of the size of the pulpit, the hardness of the pews, or the number of degrees behind the name.

## Pardon Me, but It's about These Problems

The Chair-of-Theology Approach has three main problems.

First, the basic prerequisite of spiritual maturity is short-circuited. A student's personal submission to the authority of the Word of God is confused with submission to a teacher.

Second, if for any one of a number of reasons a student turns off a teacher, the *influence line* of the Word of God is erased.

Third, when a teacher is removed from a student's life, the influence of the Word may go too. If the student goes away to college or moves to a new locality, will the Bible's influence go with him? Will he lose his faith?

Amazing, isn't it, the number of relocated families that somehow never regain their level of active involvement in church life. Some leave the Bible influence behind, as they would extra casserole dishes, outmoded clothes, or a worn stuffed chair.

### Practice While You Teach—5

Concept: *The Chair-of-Theology Approach draws excessive attention to the teacher.* Use these points to evaluate your approach to teaching.

1. *How do you respond to this statement? Why?*
"One of the most gratifying things about being a teacher is the respect that comes from being considered knowledgeable of the Bible."
agree strongly     agree     disagree     disagree strongly

2. I help my students to feel confident in their ability to understand the Bible by . . . (Complete the sentence.)

3. When I am complimented on my Bible knowledge I . . . (Complete the sentence.)

4. *How do you respond to this statement? Why?*
"As a teacher, I should take substantial portions of my teaching time for fellowship in order to get to know my students."
agree strongly     agree     disagree     disagree strongly

5. My students see me as a model of what the Bible teaches when I . . . (Complete the sentence.)

## The Teachable-Teacher Approach

The majority of interviewers at that Phoenix, Arizona seminar heard descriptions of the Bible-as-a-Club and Theology-Chair teaching.

Only two teens related a refreshing difference. Only two described situations in which an adult leader personally guided them in their own discovery of biblical truth.

"In Sunday School we were studying what Paul said about families getting along. And I couldn't believe it. He let us talk. Then we read some verses together from the Bible. He asked us questions, like what the verses said and what we thought they meant. It made us see that the Bible really does have answers. It was the neatest thing to read the Bible and find things for myself."

One boy told us about his Sunday School class. Scriptures they had discussed made him concerned about his unclean thoughts and bad vocabulary.

"I really knew it was wrong, but I didn't know how to change. That's why I went to my Sunday School teacher. He told me this was a temptation lots of people have, but that didn't make it right. He showed me this verse in Corinthians about God providing a way for us to escape any temptation. We decided to both pray about it for a week, asking God to help me find the escape. It really worked."

A careful look at diagram 9 reveals an important relationship between a teacher, students, and the Word of God.

In this situation the Word is clearly recognized as the final authority. A student and teacher together come to the Word of God with honesty and openness about their own needs. The authority of the Word is accepted over these areas of need.

The concept of a teacher swinging his Bible as a club is gone.

The image of a teacher as the final authority perched on the chair of theology is forgotten.

Instead, a teacher ministers as an equal; an equal with a different role, but equal.

A teacher becomes a model of the Word working in a life.

It is often quoted, "A message prepared in a mind will reach a

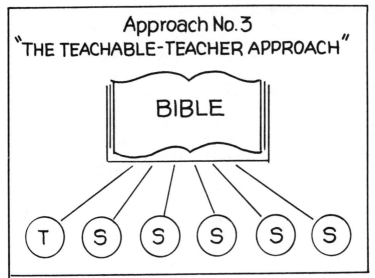

Approach No. 3
"THE TEACHABLE-TEACHER APPROACH"

BIBLE

T  S  S  S  S  S

DIAGRAM 9

mind; a message prepared in a life will reach a life."

This is the heart of the third approach.

### Straight Circles and Bent Rows

Important comment: Diagram 9 is not intended to present biblical seating arrangements.

Yes, a teacher may be up front. Or a class may sit in a circle on the floor. Platform or no platform. He can put them in straight circles or bent rows if he chooses. That's not the point.

Wherever he sits or stands, he must be sure that the class understands that all are on common ground before the Word.

### You Never Outgrow Your Need for Milk

"Like newborn babes, long for the pure milk of the Word" (1 Peter 2:2) is not a royal command for students only. Teachers are obligated too. You never outgrow your need for milk.

One vital element in Bible teaching is to admit that need openly and honestly. We must avoid projecting the image of an authority who has "arrived."

## What about Authority?

The New Testament model of authoritative proclamation is not set aside. We teach with authority, but we do not have authority in the same sense that Jesus, or even the Apostles, had authority. Our authority is the Bible. Our greatest display of authority is seen in our open submission to the authority of that Book.

In turn, it is the task of a teacher to take his students with him in a venture into God's authoritative Book. In this capacity, a teacher carefully studies the Scripture and responds in personal obedience. Then he plans ways to involve his students in the learning process. As he does, he achieves the basic goal of Bible teaching.

## The Goal: Independent Dependence

The basic goal of Bible teaching is to lead a student to a place of independent dependence upon the Word of God.

This is the point of 2 Timothy 2:2: "And the things which you have heard from me in the presence of many witnesses, these entrust to faithful men, who will be able to teach others also." A similar thought is conveyed in Hebrews 5:12: "For though by this time you ought to be teachers, you have need again for some one to teach you the elementary principles of the oracles of God, and you have come to need milk and not solid food."

The way to teaching others is the way of independent dependence on the Word. Until a Christian is capable of standing on his own understanding, how can he teach?

The goal for a teacher and his students is independent (no people as props) dependence (utter submission) before the Word of God.

## An Inductively-Deductive Approach

The Teachable-Teacher approach is both deductive and inductive. Or better, *inductively deductive*.

It is deductive in conviction; that is, the Word of God is recognized as absolute truth. Teacher and student are involved together in learning God's previously revealed truth.

It is inductive in method; namely, within the framework of the

Bible's authority, teacher and student *are* discovering together. As brothers and sisters they are bringing their lives under the authority of the Word. An atmosphere of discovery is thus created in the class, that feeling of learning together.

The teacher has studied; his preparation has been thorough; his convictions are strong; but his attitude is gracious and loving. He seeks to lead others to respond to the Word without inundating them with pressure to conform to his viewpoint.

A teachable teacher veils the dogmatism of his personal viewpoints in order firmly to establish the Word of God as the final authority. He affirms that his personal opinion is unimportant, compared with that final authority. He does this not out of weakness of conviction, but as part of a strategy of involvement.

In consideration of the greater goal of his students' independent dependence on the Bible, he teaches like a guide leading a venture of discovery in learning.

Then, having led the class to an understanding of what the Word teaches, he models before the class dogmatic acceptance of that which the Bible teaches.

### Theoretical Extremes

In one sense we are looking at theoretical extremes. Few teachers will consistently use any one approach. There may be a little of the Bible-as-a-Club in the best of them. And it's certain that the most humble of teachers often fights the temptation to climb up on that chair of theology.

But God is good and gracious, and uses us in spite of ourselves.

### There Are Advantages

Teaching as a teachable teacher does have its distinct advantages.

A student is led to bring his life under the authority of the Word of God, rather than a teacher's authority, or the press of a peer group.

Rather than being intimidated by the scholarship and academic attainments of a teacher, a student develops a healthy self-image as he learns that he can understand the Word himself and can share it with others.

This pattern of learning is a student's open door to continuing growth even if a teacher is taken out of the picture for some reason.

In the third approach, a teacher is not so interested in building up his own ego by causing others to look to him as an authority. He is genuinely interested in their spiritual maturity. He is, in fact, planning for it.

## Private Raptures: Superintendent's Nightmare

Here's an imaginary illustration: What if Sunday School teachers were raptured privately, before their fellow believers? There, caught up into the Third Heaven, *their* lot is bliss. But tune in on the travail of their students and the Sunday School Superintendent.

The superintendent spends all day Saturday attempting to round up substitute teachers. He spends the early morning hours on Sunday picking the songs for substantially extended opening exercises. All week he schedules Christian films for the next four Sundays while he recruits and trains a new staff. And what of the plight of the students?

Students whose teacher used the Bible-as-a-Club approach have lost their conscience. Students whose teacher used the Chair-of-Theology approach have lost their enlightenment. Students whose teacher used the Teachable-Teacher approach have gained one more incentive for growth. They are the new teachers in training.

## Beam and Mote: A Cautionary Note

It is much easier to apply the Word to others than to ourselves. A Teachable Teacher has learned the importance of being a model of the Word working in a life. He responds to Scripture's authority.

This should not imply that the convictions of such a teacher are weaker. They may even be stronger. People want to see our convictions, know our beliefs.

But rather than clubbing people with the Word, or dazzling them with our scholarship, truth is modeled through a teachable teacher.

Maybe this is partly what James meant when he cautioned:

"Let not many of you become teachers, my brethren, knowing that as such we shall incur a stricter judgment" (James 3:1).

The words of Christ seem uniquely appropriate: "And why do you look at the speck in your brother's eye, but do not notice the log that is in your own eye? Or how can you say to your brother, 'Let me take the speck out of your eye,' and behold, the log is in your own eye? You hypocrite, first take the log out of your own eye; and then you will see clearly enough to take the speck out of your brother's eye" (Matt. 7:3-5).

Teachable Teachers who spot their own weaknesses first can see more clearly how to help others. Teachers who thus model the Word working in their lives are desperately needed in our classrooms and pulpits today.

## Practice While You Teach—6

Concept: *The Teachable-Teacher Approach often leads students to independent dependence on the Word of God.*

Use these points to evaluate your approach to teaching.

1. *"Let not many of you become teachers, my brethren, knowing that as such we shall incur a stricter judgment" (James 3:1).* When I read this verse I feel . . . *(Complete the sentence.)*

2. *How do you respond to this statement? Why?*

"It is appropriate for teachers to share their faults and shortcomings with their students because in this way they can demonstrate their own need for the Word of God."

agree strongly     agree     disagree     disagree strongly

3. I can make definite plans for my students to stand on their own understanding of the Bible by . . . *(Complete the sentence.)*

4. When teaching controversial subjects, my students can easily sense my gracious and loving attitude, even toward those with whom I disagree.

always     usually     sometimes     seldom     never

5. My students normally have opportunity to share what they learn in my class, or in their personal study by:

"I just want my class of third grade boys to
glow—and I mean <u>really</u> glow—with
a realization of the goodness of God which
has been manifested to us-ward who believe.
Yea, verily!"

# 3

# Aim at Something or You've Aimed at Nothing

**Principle 3:** *Your teaching will be more effective if you direct it toward specific, measurable learning aims.*

One foggy February day the public school's buzzer system sliced the morning mist. The children scattered. Thirty-seven little containers of unbelievable energy crowded through the doors of room 4. There, as was the tradition, they encountered the stern gaze of Miss Marcia Johnson, their second-grade teacher.

As the preclass confusion subsided and preliminaries were completed, the middle-aged Miss Marcia mustered her most enthusiastic voice.

"Class," she said, "today is an exciting day! Today we learn about money!"

Even as she spoke, her roving eye fastened on little Danny Sullivan. He was already fidgeting.

"And even money won't excite him?" she queried herself.

How much easier it had been only ten short years ago.

"Hard to compete with Sesame Street," she told her colleagues.

Two doors down the hall Mrs. Beth Riley was teaching the school's other section of second graders. She, too, had discovered the proverb "A stern look solveth some disorders."

But this morning her mind was quite preoccupied with her task. And her students knew it.

"Today let's learn about money!" she told them.

Both teachers share the same goal, teaching their class about coin values and counting money. Both teach second graders, but

49

each approaches the task differently, with different aims, and each will experience different results.

Marcia's plan book reads: "My aim for this class period is to teach my class about coin values and money."

Beth has set more exacting goals: "By the end of this class hour, 50 percent of my students will be able to select coins to equal a specified amount of money with 80 percent accuracy."

When the teaching is completed, the students are home, and the results are evaluated, over which teacher's performance will the densest fog hang? Who is more accountable?

A few years ago a thoughtful educator put the accountability pot on the front burner and flipped up the flame. Teachers have been boiling ever since.

The issue? "To what extent is a school district entitled to demand a measurable product in student knowledge as a condition for a teacher's employment?"

Boiled down to the basics, the question is: "If a student has not learned, has the teacher really taught?"

To be sure, the public school teachers' accountability broth may bubble more fervently because of heated political issues and secondary factors but it'll be a long time before the educational world simmers down.

## If You Aim at Nothing It's a Sure Hit

I lifted the stack of old, partially yellowed seminary notes and early sermons. Shuffling through the pages I noticed something that fascinated me. As a young preacher, I had been encouraged to write out an aim for every sermon I prepared. This was, I recalled, a helpful discipline.

However, frequently I have found myself in the position of a teacher with noble aspirations, good *general* goals, but virtually no *accountability*.

## A Problem of Broad and Abstract Goals

Goals are good, but it is easy to write poor goals. This is compounded by the fact that poor goals usually look so good.

What could possibly be wrong with making our aim for the

class, "to appreciate God's grace"? or, "to grasp the significance of faith"? or, "to fully understand prophetic events"?

Basically, such aims present two problems: *abstraction* and *generality.* If a lesson aim centers on something that is intangible, abstract, and hard to measure, when will the teacher know whether he has achieved his goal?

Similarly, if the goals for the class hour are too *broad,* they are self-defeating.

The purpose of goals is to point us in a proper direction, to let us know how we are progressing toward our objective, and to send us a little signal of success when we have arrived.

Goals can do that, but not if they are broad and abstract.

"Aim at nothing," some may say, "and you'll hit it every time."

Which brings one to the point of a problem, and the horns of a dilemma. So much of the material that Sunday School teachers teach *is* abstract.

How does one measure a student's understanding of the love of God, for instance? And isn't it legitimate for the class to appreciate, *really* appreciate, the goodness of the grace of God manifested toward us?

Yea, verily. But before we climb out of the accountability pot, there are some morsels to munch on that will give more meaning to aims.

### The Gotta-Get-Through-My-Quarterly-By-Noon Syndrome

I've always been enamored with melodrama. Here's an update on the old car-racing-the-train-to-the-crossing scenario.

The engineer nervously glances over his left shoulder to the highway below. Relentlessly, a Chevy van keeps pace. Noticing the crossing ahead, the engineer frantically grips a cord and the shrill whistle violently tears a ragged edge of piercing sound above the dull driving roar of the northbound freight train.

Twenty yards away, on a ruffled ribbon of narrow asphalt, the tall beige van rumbles toward the crossing. The clammy hands of the thrill-intoxicated driver grip the wheel. A large, determined patent leather boot grinds the tortured accelerator pedal.

In a suspense snapping moment, the van lurches past a weathered white and black marker and across the glistening steel tracks. Instantly the enormous engine and its 86 freight cars flash past the crossing, creating a strobe-light effect as the late afternoon sun breaks through between the freight cars.

Strangely satisfied, the van driver decreases his speed and peers in his rearview mirror, gratified that he won the race, yet curiously questioning what he has accomplished.

And for some, Bible teaching is such a race. The concerned and determined teacher and his vanload of truth race the locomotive clock and its engineering superintendent.

## Goals: Maturity or Material?

Someone deftly expressed himself when he commented, "We teach people, not lessons."

What's the goal for a class session? To cover the next four pages, or six verses, or 19 chapters? To beat the clock?

Is the focus of goals the *material* to be presented to people or the *maturity* to be achieved in people?

If the ultimate goal is learning, what enduring result has been achieved by racing the clock, covering the content and running on to church, or home, panting from the pace?

I have never met a publisher of Sunday School curriculum who expected teachers to cover all the material. I have met many teachers, however, who feel they've failed if they haven't.

Just what should teachers be accountable for?

## Up to Your Ears in Alligators

When California public school educators found themselves on a collision course with the accountability question, a wise sage coined the phrase, "When you are up to your ears in alligators, don't forget you were sent here to drain the swamp."

It doesn't require great plateaus of imagination to attach meaning to the alligators. Many teachers saw their students in a new light, I'm sure. But there's something more profound here.

That quaint little proverb was the necessary comic relief in the pinch of the accountability drama.

Willing, and unwilling, disciples of the new campaign even

found themselves introduced to a mascot. An alligator, naturally. His name was Smirt.

Predictably, Smirt's very name was significant. Smirt proclaimed to the educational world the necessity of learning aims that were specific, measurable, identifiable, relative, and terminal.

*Specific* Broad generalities just would not cut it. "If," Smirt might inquire, "your aims are broadly-worded, how will you know if you're hitting them?" Fine question.

*Measurable* "But you must also know to what *extent* you have succeeded," Smirt would add. "Word your aims to reflect not only success or failure, but the degree of your success or failure, as well."

*Identifiable* Smirt persisted, "It is also mandatory that you frame your statement of learning objectives in such a way that you (and the rest of us) can *see* whether you have really succeeded."

*Relative* Here Smirt showed his awareness that all students are not stamped from the same mold. "Learning objectives should be worded in such a manner that you may, shall we say, grade *yourself* on the class' curve." Not every student will attain an equal level of understanding. This must be reflected in the way learning objectives are written.

*Terminal* Smirt terminated his lecture, figuratively speaking, by reminding public school teachers to include a cutoff date. "Goals must also tell you, or at least imply, when you'll arrive and evaluate your success."

"And remember," he subtly warned, "we have long waiting lists for teaching positions." Maybe there was deep significance in the fact that Smirt concluded with a discussion on "termination."

## California Smarts from Smirt
The result was predictable. Teachers pined away while planning to drain the swamp. Even good teachers complained that they had little time to perform once the arduous task of lesson planning was completed. The pretest/posttest prospect petrified many teachers.

But, you must admit, there was greater teacher accountability.

"By the end of this unit of study [Terminal], 50% of my students [Relative] will be able to select coins [Identifiable] to equal a specified amount of money [Specific] with 80% accuracy [Measurable]."

Whether considered a virus or a virtue, the accountability emphasis has spread. There are quite a number of educators who are convinced that when too many students fail, their teacher earns the "F." And a new job.

## Sunday School Teachers: Pass/Fail or Grade on a Curve?

Should the church grade its teachers, or should Smirt stay at school?

There are some built-in barriers that make it precarious to peer at pastors or people, calling for the same level of accountability among church educators that exists among public school teachers.

There are other elements, however, that indicate we should demand more of Christian educators. For instance, the "something" we should be aiming at.

### Practice While You Teach—7

Concept: *If you aim at nothing it's a sure hit.*
Use these points to evaluate your teaching aims.

1. I consciously think about the goals, the lesson aims, while I am preparing and teaching my lesson.
*always      usually      sometimes      seldom      never*

2. When I am planning to deal with a certain amount of material during a class session and a class member asks questions that are off the subject I . . . *(Complete the sentence.)*

3. I know I am a success as a teacher when . . . *(Complete the sentence.)*

4. Other people know I am a success as a teacher when . . . *(Complete the sentence.)*

5. If I wanted my class to understand the meaning of the bread and cup in 1 Corinthians 11, I could state that in the form of a specific measurable goal by phrasing it: "By the end of this class hour, most of my students will be able to" . . . *(Complete the sentence.)*

## What's the Something We Should Be Aiming At?

One foggy Sunday in February, the church's chimes sounded, and a half-melodious clanging filtered through the chilly mist. Cars were already arriving, headlights shining through the morning fog in enlarged circles of diffused light.

Children chased each other around the tables in the Sunday School classrooms and up and down the gray-green linoleum hallways.

As order gradually emerged from chaos, a dozen or two classes convened. Teachers, some confident, some frazzled, took to their posts and began their weekly trek through a previously determined passage of study.

And for a few minutes on that Sunday morning the spiritual pilgrimage of a church full of typical Christian people was shared by Sunday School teachers with varying levels of training, ability, and interest.

Later that afternoon a young woman cries over her frustration and thwarted attempts at gaining the upper hand in her class of fifth grade boys.

Another silently questions the value of trying to teach anything spiritual to 2s and 3s, but remembers the positive feedback from a young couple thrilled by their daughter's first attempts at prayer. She learned at church. In that class.

A junior high teacher throws in the towel.

A teacher of senior citizens goes home rewarded by a kind comment and a squeezed-hand-thank you.

And the Sunday School superintendent calls the pastor, apologizes for interrupting his roast and vegetables, and pours out his exasperation and disillusionment. Teachers are scarce.

What's it all about? Spiritual maturity is involved, but the problem is more specific, measurable, and identifiable.

### Tri-, Di-, or Uni-

Seminary life is famous for its theological discussions. Sub- and supralapsarianism; post-, pre-, and amillenialism, parsing and conjugations—curious things done with words in biblical languages.

The discussion of trichotomy versus dichotomy is one of these age-old theological questions. "Is man composed of three parts, or two?" Is it "body, soul, and spirit?" Or, "body and soul-spirit?"

Once, in the midst of such a discussion, I interrupted—a very rude thing to do—and declared that I was a *unichotomist,* that I believed man consisted of *one* part. My humor was mistaken for gross ignorance by one fellow seminarian. Another smiled. A third agreed.

And, of course, the point is that we minister to whole people, not chopped up bundles of spirit, and soul, mind and emotions, carried about in a gunny sack of flesh and sinew. And as we teach, we teach real people. Whole people. This should affect our goals in teaching.

## The Need to Heed

Bible teachers always hope that their teaching will be heeded. They hope people will think, feel, and act differently as a result of their teaching.

This is not just egocentricity, though it may sometimes degenerate to that. We, as teachers of the Bible, are communicating an authoritative document, a message from God about life and how it is to be lived.

At this point we legitimately differ from the person who is teaching other facts, a public school teacher, for example. "All truth is God's truth." True. But the Bible is the only direct revelation of God's truth entrusted to us.

Good Bible teachers get very concerned about how their teaching is received. They do not deviate from the message because someone gets a bit ruffled, but they do care. It's kind of like Jesus weeping over Jerusalem. Bible teachers are result-oriented inasmuch as they never lose sight of the goal of changed lives. When lives don't change, lamentation is in order.

And when lives don't change, sometimes the fault is with the hearer. Often it is with the teacher. Good goals are, therefore, mandatory. It helps to know where we are to go, how we are progressing toward that goal, and if and when we arrive at our goal. That's where learning aims come in.

## Teaching for Feeling

A lot of teaching, preaching and coffee cup counseling is less than it could be because of a wrong emphasis on emotions. That's understandable. After all, a person cannot *see* the Holy Spirit. It seems natural to insist on clearly identifying His work. And what is more obvious in us and in others than our emotions?

Someone cries. He appears repentant for some wickedness or bitterness in his life. It's easy to assume the Spirit has worked. Maybe He has, but there is a subtle peril in the propensity to confuse means with the end.

"If only I can make them weep, I am assured the Lord has worked."

"If I can coax them down the aisle, I'll know the Spirit did it."

"If only I can pressure him into a profession of faith . . . 'The Lord's doing, marvelous in our eyes!' "

The problem is that there are a lot of things that make people feel like crying. And, to borrow from the absurd, it is not the Holy Spirit that drives people into deep dedication to false causes. Many will say "Lord, Lord" who have never really met Him.

*Feeling* is not a flawless gauge. Emotional response is not a guarantee of divine work. We should develop the patience required to wait for the clear evidence of a changed life.

On the other hand, our teaching should assail the conscience. People should feel it. Emotions *are* involved. Our teaching is more than throwing out so many facts.

We talk, and properly so, of *inspiration aims,* an appeal to the *emotions.* But at the same time, we understand that these inspiration aims cannot be separated from the content that is presented.

## Lives to Be Changed

The preacher stepped to the pulpit. It was his final message in a special series on Peter's second epistle. Again he reminded the congregation, "God wants men and women of *faith!"*

And just what is a man or a woman of faith?

"A man of faith amends his life in favor of revelation!" The core of apostasy is that heart of unbelief that motivates a person to stand off from revelation.

Every time a Christian approaches the Bible he has an obligation to be open to changing. He must change his life to bring it into conformity with what the Word teaches.

That's what is involved in being men and women of faith.

And preachers and teachers are aiming for that response in the people they teach. Teaching and learning that stop short of changed lives quickly turn, chameleon-like, to legalism and Pharisee-Christianity.

Cold, calculating pursuit of factual information without the continual evaluation of Scripture's demands on the student's life-style falls far short of the purpose of Scripture itself.

"How can a young man keep his way pure?" the psalmist asks. He immediately answers, "By keeping it according to Thy Word" (119:9).

The Apostle Paul told carnal Corinthians about the Old Testament, "Now these things happened as examples for us, that we should not crave evil things, as they also craved" (1 Cor. 10:6).

"All Scripture is inspired by God and profitable," Paul explained to Timothy, "for teaching, for reproof, for correction, for training in righteousness; that the man of God may be adequate, equipped for every good work" (2 Tim. 3:16-17).

And so, legitimately, we speak of *conduct-response aims,* (an appeal to the will). Note, however, that changed conduct and an appeal to the will cannot stand independent of the content to be presented.

## They Spare the Rod and Use Behavior Mod

Those who are committed to *behavior modification* are seeking to change the values and attitudes of their students through education. Behavior modification is scary business in the hands of non-Christian educators.

On the other hand, changed lives (behavior modification) must always be the objective of those who teach Bible truth (see chapter 1). The formulation and pursuit of a specific conduct-response aim is a direct step toward that style of Bible teaching.

## Plenty of Verses

The church where it happened is known throughout the evangelical world. The teacher (in this case the youth pastor) did have a goal. Word had reached him the week before that some of the best products of his "hard-line fundamentalist" teaching had backslidden into listening to the local hard rock radio station.

This was not the time for more Bible study, he reasoned. This was the time to call a halt to sin. This was the time to zero in on changed behavior patterns.

"There are plenty of verses," he said, "that I could use this morning, but I'll not take the time to do that. I just want you to know how ashamed I am that you're letting me down by slipping back into habits of sinful behavior."

That which followed was an eloquent plea, clearly aimed at changing the behavior of his students.

One may sympathize with his decision to aim that Sunday's lesson toward changing the conduct of his students. But his approach has problems.

Though it would be more difficult for him, he needed to discipline himself to identify specific areas of Bible knowledge his students needed. Holiness of life must spring from a proper knowledge of, and response to, Scripture.

When we circumvent scriptural knowledge in our attempts to change people's lives, our teaching degenerates to cheap manipulation and legalism.

## As You Know, So Shall You Go (Sort Of)

Film producer Ken Anderson, in developing his Successful Christian Living Seminar, sought to underscore a basic life-changing principle: "To act like a Christian you must first learn to think like a Christian."

That's the precise point that Jesus was pointing at when He spoke of the "heart."

"The good man out of the good treasure of his heart brings forth what is good; and the evil man out of the evil treasure brings forth what is evil; for his mouth speaks from that which fills his heart" (Luke 6:45).

Heart. The word suggests sentimental, emotional images.
"I love you with all my heart."
"My heart is breaking."
Or even, "Have a heart!"
In Central Africa they speak of the liver as the center of emotional activity. A small cultural difference exists, then, between a broken heart and a bent liver. The Africans have liver. The Americans have heart.

But that's not what Jesus meant. He was not saying, "Let your emotional frame rule." He was not even saying, "Let your conscience be your guide." The Jews understood Him. When they thought "emotions" they aimed lower than the heart, but when they spoke of the "heart" they had thinking in mind. When Jesus spoke of "the heart" He had reference to the intentions, the purposes, the designs and thoughts of the inner man.

Jesus was saying that what you fill your mind with is going to issue in the kind of life you lead. "To act godly," we might paraphrase Him, "you must first learn to think godly."

That's why Paul talked about a "renewing of the mind" (Rom. 12:2). And that's why we speak of *knowledge aims* (an appeal to the *mind*).

## The Fact, Faith, Feeling Express

The issue is not unlike Campus Crusade's "fact, faith, feeling express." The caboose is optional.

A person begins with *facts*. God said it. They believe it. There's *faith*. Emotions may be high, or not so high. They follow along behind, caboose-style. That's the proper place for *feelings*. If we think of it in terms of learning aims, we can structure a similar model.

Those who begin with, or place undue emphasis on, emotions are on the wrong track.

Those who attempt to change conduct without deep interaction with the Word of God have switched to legalism and manipulation.

Those who take Scripture knowledge as the beginning point for life-changing teaching are in a position to have real success in

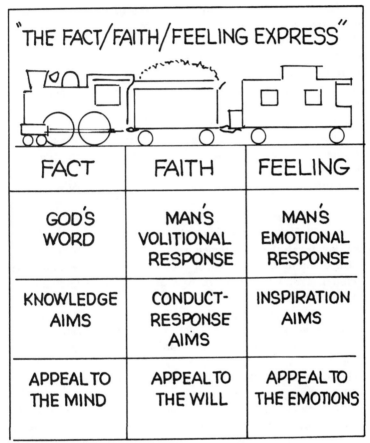

| FACT | FAITH | FEELING |
|------|-------|---------|
| GOD'S WORD | MAN'S VOLITIONAL RESPONSE | MAN'S EMOTIONAL RESPONSE |
| KNOWLEDGE AIMS | CONDUCT-RESPONSE AIMS | INSPIRATION AIMS |
| APPEAL TO THE MIND | APPEAL TO THE WILL | APPEAL TO THE EMOTIONS |

DIAGRAM 10

formulating and achieving conduct-response and inspiration aims. Knowledge of scriptural truth always comes first.

### Practice While You Teach—8

Concept: *What's the "something" we should be aiming at?*
Use these points to evaluate your teaching aims.

1. When students in my class do not make changes in their lives that I know they need to make I . . . *(Complete the sentence.)*

2. My students would be more likely to change their lives in response to my teaching if . . . (Complete the sentence.)

3. In my teaching, students may be led to an emotional response without fully understanding scriptural knowledge.

always     usually     sometimes     seldom     never

4. I know that the Holy Spirit has used my teaching when . . . (Complete the sentence.)

5. How do you respond to this statement? Why?

"If my students change in response to my teaching, but cannot explain to someone else, from the Bible, why they changed, I have manipulated them."

agree strongly     agree     disagree     disagree strongly

## Somehow Aims Always Point Back to You

I determined that today would be different. Today I'd discover just how much the class remembered from our study.

On different sheets of paper I wrote the words, Rapture, Millennium, Tribulation, Church Age, and Return in Glory. Having resisted the common "Class, you'll remember we've been studying" introduction, I promptly selected five volunteers. They came to the front of the class. I gave each one a sheet of paper.

There they stood, in jumbled order, each holding a sheet of paper.

I turned to the class. "OK, arrange them in order, according to the way we've been studying."

I felt awkward and accountable. I had been challenged to evaluate my success in teaching on the basis of what they had learned. It had been easy to feel successful because I had shared good stuff. Or because they had been impressed with my understanding of eschatology.

I thought I did well. My lecture was clear enough. But they failed. They just could not do it. They recalled having heard all the terms, but they could not think it through on their own. They agreed with my viewpoint; they just couldn't remember what it was!

It was a turning point in my approach to teaching when I admitted that their failure to learn meant I had failed to teach.

I still wanted my class to really understand the glorious things that God the Lord has prepared for them, and the tremendous cataclysmic events about to break over this world of ours at any moment, suddenly, when the apocalyptic age comes and the eschatological unfolding of events begins.

My long-range goals for their maturity and Bible learning had not diminished; I'm sure they increased. But I became more aware of specific, measurable learning aims that were realistic and attainable. These goals became the focus of my teaching during a given class hour.

## On Scratching and Itching

Prof was noted for his carefully supported, graciously firm dogmatism. He was the kind of teacher who was mildly irritated by chit-chatty students who cornered him for coffee and coke conversations about fine doctrinal points, without a pen and paper.

He was available, sure. But he viewed time and theology the same way, both as stewardships. Why consume time asking questions if we don't really care?

An unfortunate student once asked the ultimate question, "Why don't we study stuff that's more 'practical'?"

Asking a theology prof if doctrine is practical is like questioning a Hebrew teacher concerning the importance of the Old Testament. Prof, noticeably restraining himself and avoiding lengthy sermonizing, simply responded, "It's not just my job to scratch where it itches. It's my job to scratch where it may someday itch."

The inquirer, lost in the enigma, missed the significance of the moment.

We identify an itch and scratch like mad. Simultaneously, vigilantly, and systematically, we scratch also where it may someday itch. We are whole-counsel-of-God people.

Specific, measurable learning aims lead us to the freedom of this balance.

## Lofty Goals for Tired Souls

It was a representative teacher who said, "I want my class to really, and I mean *really,* appreciate the goodness of the grace of God manifested to us-ward."

This is a noble aspiration, a biblical passion, but a poor learning goal.

How does a teacher determine his level of effectiveness in leading his class to appreciate the glorious goodness of God's grace? How does he measure it? That aim carries with it so little accountability, it would be easy to hide behind.

An observable tendency often emerges. The higher and more noble a goal sounds, the less valid it may be—an inverse proportion.

The more elevated and religious-sounding an aim, the less attainable it may be and the less accountable the teacher may feel.

Lofty goals for tired souls. Although our long-range objectives are lofty, in the most celestial sense of the word, those long-range, lofty objectives are best realized as we teach with good, down-to-earth learning aims which are specific, measurable, and open to teacher accountability.

## Accountability and Self-Judgment

The teacher begins with a realistically formulated Bible knowledge aim. The anticipated change of behavior is stated in a conduct-response aim which flows logically from the teaching of that Scripture, or scriptural concept. The appropriate corresponding attitude, or feeling, is expressed as an inspiration aim.

That is the model of Bible-centered learning aims. Like the train: fact—Bible knowledge, faith—willingness to change, feeling—emotional response.

A heavy load of accountability rides on that style of teaching, though no teacher of biblical truth can escape the principle of accountability anyway. For instance, *why* are we teaching?

There are inner recesses of our motives that are hard for us to fully discern. Yet even for these we are accountable to the Lord.

And there are other questions: *What* are we teaching? *How* are we teaching?

We are responsible to use the best, most effective methods of preparation and presentation we are capable of using.

Teaching with specific, measurable learning aims gives a lot of help in these important realms of teaching responsibility.

It's sort of like judging ourselves, that we be not judged.

## Practice While You Teach—9

Concept: *Somehow aims always point back to you.*

Use these points to evaluate your teaching aims.

1. *I will evaluate my success in teaching on the basis of what my students learn.*

If I were to set that standard for myself as a teacher, I would know my students had learned when . . . (Complete this sentence.)

2. *They agree with my viewpoint, they just don't remember what it is.*

That statement could accurately be made of my class.

always    usually    sometimes    seldom    never

3. In my teaching ministry, in order to "scratch where it may someday itch" I . . . (Complete the sentence.)

4. I teach because . . . (Complete the sentence.)

5. *Complete the following statement by selecting a, b, or c.*

If I were going to write my own lesson aims for a particular passage of Scripture I would begin with

(a) an inspiration aim        (b) a knowledge aim

(c) a conduct-response aim

"Now in the 34th place note something
intriguing: it says here,
'Moses lifted up his eyes . . .'
If you'll just stay with me for a few more minutes
I'll be able to complete all 37 points. . . ."

# 4

# Don't Just Teach!
# Help "Them" Learn

**Principle 4:** *Your teaching will be more effective if you reinforce the lesson with student participation in Guided Discovery Learning.*

I reclined momentarily in the tattered green desk chair. It was that dull, office-furniture green that somehow fails to lift your spirits on Monday mornings. My hands subconsciously slid across the shabby armrests. The chair creaked.

I picked at the patches of worn vinyl on the loose armrests. The wood was beginning to show through.

*This really does need to be replaced,* I thought to myself, tightening a loose screw under the left armrest with my fingers.

I wrestled my wandering mind back to the project sprawling across my desk: Creative teaching methods, and techniques to involve the learner. *Sometimes ideas flow,* I mused. *Other times they are sticky blobs of creative goop that barely ooze onto the typewritten page in time to satisfy the printer's deadline schedule.*

*Will teachers use this idea?* I asked myself. *Perhaps it should be simpler.*

There was a knock at the door. I sat up abruptly. The chair's backrest clunked against its cold steel frame. It was someone delivering the mail.

I mumbled a cordial "Thank you."

Back to lesson 10. Just then a letter caught my eye.

"So could you please recommend some material on new teaching methods. I feel like I'm getting into a rut out here."

It was from a missionary in France for whom I had long had

67

high respect and deep admiration. I couldn't help contrasting his warm personal letter with two other letters in my file.

Encouraged, the ideas began to flow, interrupted intermittently, though less frequently, by my tacky pensiveness.

## Riddle Me This

The riddle is reality.

*Question:* "Why do Sunday School teachers teach the way they do?"

*Answer:* "Because it's the way they were taught."

Profound? Perhaps not. But there's a strong fiber of truth in this conundrum.

If we liberate our imagination and assume it's true, the problems we inherit are legion.

## The World's Worst Teaching Method

"The worst teaching method," it has been said, "is the one we use all the time."

It's not that the method is bad. Variety is the spice of more than just life; it adds a unique flavor to teaching, too.

If I have used the same teaching method every Sunday of my adult life, that may be the worst possible method for me to use this Sunday.

Teachers do tend to teach the way they were taught; not even, we might add, the way they were taught to teach.

There's the rub. Many teacher-training courses are lectures against the lecture method. There is a formidable barrier to overcome.

## The Seven Last Words of the Church

The seven last words of the church are not: "Occupy till I come." They are: "But we've never done it that way before!"

An otherwise sterling church can board up the doors when that mind-set grips the church. When teachers adopt that philosophy, it may be that they should occupy themselves at tasks other than teaching.

## Life Is a Pendulum

It's hard to maintain balance when we are striving to reach something. It is sometimes illusive to be "in."

*Exhibit A:* The weary youth pastor looked wistfully at his wife after a party with the church kids. He had made it his consuming passion to be "with it."

"Just when I finally find out where it's at," he sighs, "somebody moves it."

And so it often is with teaching methods. We find one we are comfortable with and we ride it to death. We are creatures of extremes.

### Lecture Only: Teacher Knows Best

Glancing across the mildly cluttered living room, the representative teacher can be seen, slouching in a reclining chair. Ten feet away the television blares. The father-turned-teacher seems unphased except when a rumble of canned laughter chuckles out of the television speaker system. That had always annoyed him, even when he was not concentrating on other things.

Stretched out on the carpet, the two boys and their schnauzer, Prince, remain transfixed, glued to the tube. Mom sits on the couch, as usual, somehow simultaneously reading *Woman's Day,* working on an embroidery kit, watching the program, and interrupting her husband. He's studying for his Sunday School lesson.

The pattern of Saturday night family life contributed to his already strong bent toward last minute preparation. When it came to Sunday School lessons, he was a late Saturday night man.

By the time Sunday morning's moment of truth had arrived, the representative teacher had read the section of Scripture to be covered. He had read the curriculum materials and prepared what he could prepare at the last moment. He had made notes, underlined, and even "tossed 'n' turned" over it.

He had pulled his favorite commentaries off the shelf during the commercials and after he got the kids to bed. (Once or twice when he had started preparing early he had even borrowed books from the pastor.)

After all the initial work, he had reviewed, discussing it with his wife. He took a final peek Sunday morning at breakfast. Even in this less-than-ideal setting, the representative teacher learned.

But as he approached his class, this material was new to them. It was their first time through. It hit them cold or, at best, luke-warm. This disposition was admirable, their attention span ade-quate. They even learned.

But they didn't learn like *he* learned. As he taught, he was again reading, reviewing, explaining. Even for the marginally qualified teacher, the lecture method has proven itself to be one of the finest teaching methods conceivable. For the teacher.

## Teachers Get Smarter and Smarter

An enormous gap exists between the knowledge of teachers and that of their students in the typical church situation. It is the teachers who had been personally involved in study and in the mechanics of that verbal presentation.

They learn while they prepare, and they learn while they teach. The result is logical: teachers and preachers get smarter and smarter. At the same time, the general level of Bible knowl-edge in our churches may improve only slightly, remain unchanged, or even diminish.

## Engineering Quiet

We often grasp at the oddest standards for success. If a class of 15 fourth graders remains perfectly quiet and virtually motionless for 40 minutes we tend to declare ourselves victorious.

Perhaps we measure our level of attainment in an adult class by the number of pages we can read to the students before the superintendent blows the whistle.

Success in teaching teens seems readily identifiable: no shoulder punching, passing notes, snickering, or wise remarks.

But success as a Sunday School teacher is not to be measured by any of these standards.

## When Has a Teacher Taught?

At what point do we declare a teacher successful? Or, when has a teacher taught?

It was a perceptive educator who affirmed: "A teacher has not taught until the pupil has learned."

More than engineering minutes of quiet, more than reading reams of printed material, success as a teacher is measured in the product, which is learning, or the lack of it.

Even "successful" lectures may fail to produce learning, but astonishing things happen when teachers make it their objective to see students *learn,* not just "get taught."

They may even change methods.

### Lecture Only

Lecture-only teachers are the only species in captivity who manufacture their own cages. Some of these crafty communicators slip through the bars and effectively exchange ideas with their audience. For others, perhaps most, each point of the outline, each phrase spoken, may become another cold iron bar separating that teacher from his goal of student learning.

In its extreme, teacher and students may stare at one another and see only the cage. In the place of two-way communication, the teacher and students are aware only of the lesson, not of learning. That is a cage.

### Student Involvement: A Key Concept

Through carefully planned, conscientiously applied techniques to involve the student—Guided Discovery Learning—a teacher can open the gate of understanding and learning.

The actual product, Bible knowledge, may increase significantly when these simple methods and techniques are used.

### How Do We Answer the Cone?

For twenty-plus years, educators have talked about the so-called "Cone of Learning," or "Cone of Experience" (see diagram 11). The cone is an attempt to visualize graphically the concept of student involvement. Toward the top of the cone, the experiences are more abstract and indirect. "Verbal and visual symbols" is a fancy way of saying "Reading books, listening to lectures and sermons, and looking at pictures, maps, and charts."

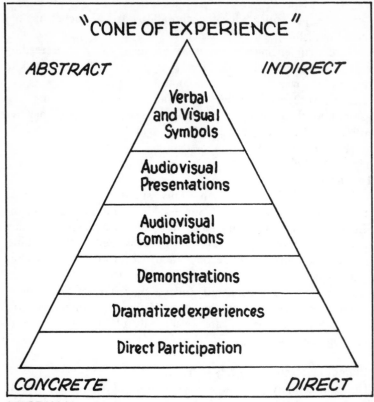

**"CONE OF EXPERIENCE"**

*ABSTRACT*  *INDIRECT*

Verbal and Visual Symbols

Audiovisual Presentations

Audiovisual Combinations

Demonstrations

Dramatized experiences

Direct Participation

*CONCRETE*  *DIRECT*

DIAGRAM 11

Until recently *verbal and visual symbols* just about summed up church education. In many, probably most, churches it still does.

Moving toward the bottom of the cone, the experiences become more concrete and direct. For example, listening to a record (which is an audio/visual presentation) is a more direct experience than reading a book (verbal/visual). If the teacher decides to show slides, or some pre-talkie super-eight movie footage, that classifies as audio/visual, specifically visual.

When sight and sound are *combined,* one shifts categories from audio/visual presentations to audiovisual combinations. And that is a bit more direct—television, films, slide tapes, etc. It is also more concrete.

With demonstrations, field trips, and exhibits, the student is learning by observation of some other person or thing or place. Observing in person is more direct—and concrete—than doing it vicariously, by watching a film or television.

Then there are dramatized experiences. Here the learner simulates a real life experience. This may be done through role play, skits, or simulation. Or it may be done through guided discussions, buzz groups, case studies, and such. Because of the direct student involvement, even abstract, indirect experiences become more concrete, more direct.

At the bottom of the cone is direct participation. If the student is doing it "with responsibility for the outcome," as one writer has suggested, that's direct experience. Student teaching is one example.

Thinking through the cone diagram, it becomes clear that some techniques lend themselves better to student involvement. Other methods make it easier to communicate factual material. A teacher has some variables to wrestle with, it's true. But a teacher who faces the necessity of student involvement in learning will probably grow uneasy about a lecture-only approach.

In guiding students toward learning, skillfully applied involvement techniques may often take the place of the lecture method. Or they may become the elements that will transform the dry bones of a dead lecture into a virile presentation, applicable to a student's needs.

## Practice While You Teach—10

Concept: *With the lecture method, teacher knows best.*
Use these points to evaluate your teaching methods.

1. *Think about your teaching over the past few months and then respond to this question:*
I learned to teach the way I do by . . . (*Complete the sentence.*)

2. I teach by using the lecture method:
*always    usually    sometimes    seldom    never*

3. When radically different ideas or methods are suggested to me I
. . . (*Complete the sentence.*)

4. *How do you respond to this statement? Why?*

"Teachers who lecture almost exclusively are reluctant to change because they feel it is the most effective method."
*agree strongly      agree      disagree      disagree strongly*
    5. *How do you respond to this statement? Why?*
"There is a relationship between boredom or discipline problems and how deeply involved the class is in the learning process."
*agree strongly      agree      disagree      disagree strongly*

## Student Involvement: They Learn More

Sunday School teachers who use mainly the lecture method are on a collision course with the pendulum of pedagogical reform.

We are creatures of extremes and pendulums swing two ways. There comes a time to duck, or at least to evaluate.

A poignant little saying illustrates the point. "I hear and I forget, I see and I remember, I do and I understand."

## What We Learn from Common Senses

Though we've all heard the "figures don't lie, but liars figure" rhetoric, we have a fascination with statistical tables.

I recall sitting through a lecture which, for the most part, had failed to arrest my attention. I noticed, however, intermittent pockets of interesting information. They pulled my attention back. Most of these pockets of interesting information were statistical. And I have found myself passing the little gems along to others.

Here's one: If we took the total sum of everything we know, what percentage of it would we have learned from each of our common senses—taste, touch, smell, hearing, sight?

*(Cover up the correct percentages and estimate. The total should equal 100 percent.)*

### How We Learn

We learn through:

| | |
|---|---|
| TASTE | 1% |
| TOUCH | 1½% |
| SMELL | 3½% |
| HEARING | 11% |
| SIGHT | 83% |

"These studies were commissioned by Socony-Vacuum Corporation and published by Xerox Corporation," the speaker said in sharing some of the other particulars. But I tuned in on those statistics. They opened my eyes a bit wider.

We may allow for a "flub factor," or assume that these figures are not *exactly* representative of our Sunday School class. However, any casually observing teacher will find them enlightening, and they may cause him to question his idealistic assumptions about his lectures.

"I hear and I forget, I see and I remember . . ." That interested me.

## What about Retention?

In our ministries of teaching/discipleship, we are interested in learning. Perhaps we should be more interested in how much is *retained*. When we're through sharing all our good material, what does the student carry out the door?

*(Cover up the correct percentages and estimate what percentage of what a person learned you would expect him to retain.)*

### What We Retain

We retain:

| | |
|---|---|
| 10% | of what we READ. |
| 20% | of what we HEAR. |
| 30% | of what we SEE. |
| 50% | of what we SEE AND HEAR. |
| 70% | of what we HEAR AND TELL. |
| 90% | of what we TELL AND DEMONSTRATE. |

The speaker shared different, though proportionate, figures for retention after three hours, and then after three days. The more fascinating observation is the parallel of these figures with the Cone of Experience (see diagram 12).

It's all predictable, but the statistical "confirmation" is intriguing.

If the table on "learning" reinforces *"I hear and I forget, I see and I remember,"* then surely the table on "retention" underscores *"I do and I understand."*

DIAGRAM 12

As I said, studies confirm it. People learn and retain significantly more when they are directly involved in learning.

## But the Figures Are in Flux

While talking to Sunday School teachers at a recent seminar, I had occasion to share those statistical observations regarding learning and retention.

At the conclusion of the session I was approached by a dear lady, a former public school teacher. She had also had a number of occasions to teach Sunday School personnel. Turning to a page in her "ubiquitous little notebook," she shared a different set of percentages. There they were, scrawled in blue ink. And she cited a source. Taste, touch, and smell percentages were about the same as the 1%, 1½%, and 3½% I had mentioned. But she rated hearing considerably higher and sight correspondingly lower.

We compared dates and the mystery was solved. Her statistics were a bit older. Today we are more "media-aware." The figures are in flux. They're not immutable. I suppose it should not surprise us that in the day of billboards and television, visual communications occupy a place of greater prominence.

We may only imagine the contours that such studies could take in another 20 years.

### Grandpa Read the Fine Print
We may retain 10 percent of what we read, but Grandpa got a higher rating. For him, awareness came primarily through print. Gramps would wade into those dense black and white pages right up to his eyeballs. And when he finished reading he began the tedious process of chewing on each argument and digesting the facts.

The end result was that awareness and decisions were based on the printed page.

### Today's Turn to the Tube
We've come a long way since Grandpa's day. Today political opinions and common awareness often come packaged in a tube, imported through a wire in our wall, having slipped in through a curious device called an antenna.

Television has drastically altered our methods of acquiring knowledge. Sunday School students are not the same either.

Teaching methods that were acceptable, or even exceptional, in Grandpa's day may not make it with today's turn to the tube.

### Discussion Isn't Necessarily a Pool of Ignorance
Teaching-learning methods which emphasize student involvement needn't be viewed with apprehension or contempt. And discussion doesn't have to be a pool of ignorance.

Contemporary Sunday School curriculums present dozens of learning activities built into the presentation of the content. These activities are not intended as time wasters. They're not just filler. They are, for the most part, a serious effort at grappling with the question, "How do people learn?"

## Involvement, Motivation, Learning

Those who teach adults are generally the most reluctant to embrace the concept of teaching through student involvement. But a very important relationship exists between involvement, motivation, and learning.

This was forcefully illustrated through a recent conversation with a Sunday School teacher. After a Saturday seminar on teaching, it was my responsibility to teach an adult Sunday School class the next day.

"These folks just don't go for that kind of thing," I was cautioned by their teacher. "They just don't discuss."

Having asked his permission to "give it a try," I opened class with a few agree-disagree questions that related to the lesson I was presenting. The class got involved. In fact, it was difficult to cut off the discussion when it was time to move on in the lesson.

Now it may be easier for a "visiting expert." If necessary the expert *can* settle down on a few good lessons and repeat them from church to church. Regardless, that class does illustrate an important concept: We cannot motivate anyone. We can stimulate, encourage, and involve, but we can't motivate.

That's something the student must bring to the process. Ultimately motivation is something the Holy Spirit generates, though we can become partners in the process through meaningful involvement.

### Practice While You Teach—11

Concept: *With student involvement they learn more.*

Use these points to evaluate how much student involvement you permit in your teaching.

1. "We learned 11 percent of what we know through the sense of hearing, 83 percent through sight."

If I assume that those figures represent even a rough approximation of how people learn, as a teacher I should . . . (Complete the sentence.)

2. Assuming that it is true that people retain about 50 percent of what they see and hear, and 70 percent of what they hear and tell, and 90 percent of what they tell and demonstrate, as a teacher I should . . . (Complete the sentence.)

3. How do you respond to the following statement? Why?
"Teaching people in a culture saturated by the media—TV, radio, billboards, magazines—poses a unique problem, and warrants, even demands, the use of new, innovative methods which may have been unnecessary even 30 years ago."
agree strongly    agree    disagree    disagree strongly

4. I follow the suggestions in my curriculum resources including the use of learning activities.
always    usually    sometimes    seldom    never

5. (a) I am most open to change when . . . (Complete the sentence.)
(b) I am most reluctant to change when . . . (Complete the sentence.)

### Balance: The Golden Mean Avoids the Extremes

Restrained zeal is a rare bird, and so is balance. Which is a different way of saying that involvement is a *means,* not an end.

A certain man who was a teacher arose one Sunday morning and went off to teach his students. And lo, it came about that his students were grievously bored and were sleeping through much of his lesson. Being mindful that the fault was not with the Scriptures he presented, the man waxed angry. And being thus angry, he purposed in his heart that he would not alter his methodology. And behold, his students sleepeth, even unto this very hour.

Now there was in that very same city another who taught Sunday School. And when it was noised abroad that the former teacher's students didst slumber, this man determined that it should not so be with him.

So he arose quite early and ventured out into the bookstores of his city. And finding a multitude of scrolls, he sat himself down to study. And while he read, behold it occurred to that man that he might indeed profit from the learning of the people. And so it came to pass that as the time continued, that man learned more and more from the people. But in the course of presenting the Scriptures with great creativity of method, that man came to be more enamored with his methodology than with the Scriptures. And being of that mind it happened that the Scriptures came to be neglected in his teaching.

Woe to that teacher! He hath sown to the methodology, and of the methodology hath reaped his reward. And his teaching hath also fallen short. And great was the fall of it.

## THEORETICAL EXTREMES TO AVOID IN SUNDAY SCHOOL TEACHING

| A GREAT LECTURE WITH NO STUDENT INVOLVEMENT | GREAT STUDENT INVOLVEMENT BUT PRACTICALLY NO CONTENT |
|---|---|
| Result: Students learn and retain practically nothing of the great content presented | Result: Students learn and retain a great percentage of the "practically nothing" that is presented |

DIAGRAM 13

### Extreme 1: Great Lecture with No Student Involvement

Assuming it were possible—these are *theoretical* extremes—to present a great lecture while at the same time having *no* student involvement, the result would be as diagrammed above. Students would learn and retain *practically nothing* in proportion to the great content presented.

Traditionally, evangelical teaching and preaching has frequently erred *in the direction* of this extreme.

### Extreme 2. Great Student Involvement but Practically No Content

The pendulum swings. As evangelicals have thought more seriously about the product of student learning, methods have been called into question. Excellent seminars and printed materials have reminded Christian educators of the priority of learning. The Church is being equipped with excellent methods to involve the student in learning. Much of this emphasis and methodology has been borrowed from secular education.

But there are pendulum perils here as well. Assuming it were possible (the extremes are still theoretical) to achieve great student involvement with virtually no content communicated, the result would be as diagrammed. Students would learn and retain a commendable percentage of the *practically nothing* that is presented.

## Backlash and Balance

Evangelicals often find themselves boarding the jet as the passengers deplane. We stuff our satchel and tote with a tolerable mixture of biblical principles and 5 to 15-year-old methods and start up the ramp. In the process we bump and jostle those who tried those methods. Maybe they abused them. In any case, they're headed for the terminal of change, often leaving some good ideas under the seat. "The newest," it was once said, "is not necessarily the truest."

Why can't we just soar with the best, balanced and buoyant? Because balance is elusive.

"It's not working in secular education. Why bring it into the Church?"

The open class concept, for example, has become the pressure point of stern criticism.

"Educational anarchy," some have suggested.

"There's no end of trouble when you become 'learner-centered.'"

And so, with gratitude, we cordially nod to those flight attendants who remind us, "There is a shelf for balance. Not just because it's moderate, but because it's right."

Activity teaching can degenerate to fun and games, sanctioning or even rewarding discipline problems. Or it can be used to teach authoritative truth, enhancing learning.

## Bide Your Time, Bite Your Tongue

"But we just don't have time for all that!"

It was the frustrated voice of a pleasant, middle-aged woman. She was floundering in the curricular sea of teaching aids. Every helpful suggestion we had thrown her way turned to a millstone of exasperation as she reflected on her available teaching time.

"Bible learning activities? Guided Discovery Learning? Great! But when?

"Involve students? I don't have time!

"Good curriculum? Yes! But how do I implement it?"

If the teacher gets it all together—and this woman seemed to—will there be conflicts with the superintendent, the pastor, or "the way things have always been done at our church"?

Bide your time. Change comes slowly. Bite your tongue. Be swift to hear and slow to speak. Exercise supreme patience. Teach, teach, teach. Do the best within the framework of your limitations.

## Earthmover Openings

Time. In our seminar ministries, lack of time is probably the complaint most frequently voiced, the frustration most often expressed.

Like an enormous yellow earthmover, Sunday School opening exercises often transport fertile, potential-packed minutes of teaching time far from the yawning crevice of need. That load of irretrievable time, so haphazardly dumped into typical Sunday School openings, is only rarely deposited near the point of concentrated study. Teaching time is so limited and yet so wasted.

## Sculptured Sessions

On a different level of educational stewardship, some churches view the total of their available time as one block. That block may not be as massive as it could be, but it is functional. From that solid slab of entrusted time, an hour, or perhaps two, a sensitive staff creatively chisels a total period of teaching. Large groups, small groups, short segments of time, longer segments, group participation, or teacher-led situations.

Each element of the total learning experience is carefully

directed from planning to completion by specific, measurable learning aims (see chapter 2).

## Meatballs or Milk?

We are "whole-counsel-of-God" people. Lamentably, the people we teach are not always ready for spaghetti and meatballs with the authenticity of genuine Italian seasonings. Some are "milk only" infants.

Biblical writers, we have previously demonstrated (chapter 1), often found it necessary to limit their message to fit the maturity level of their learners.

We will discover the same. Adding to meatballs, milk, and maturity, the concept of *methodology,* we get the question, "How does the class' maturity relate to our methods?"

When perception of the student's maturity level and of his needs is blended with the teacher's implementation of creative teaching methods, the product may be exquisite discipleship.

The essential ingredient is a warm, sharing-caring relationship with the students. That relationship makes even mediocre methodology palatable, and when that relationship is blended with the best in balanced methodology, learning becomes absolutely scrumptious.

### Practice While You Teach—12

Concept: *Balance is the golden mean that avoids the extremes.*
Use these points to evaluate the extent of balance in your teaching.

1. When it comes to change I would characterize myself as:
reckless    avant-garde    creative    open    analytical
cautious    conservative    rigid    fearful    petrified

2. I *approach* the extreme of having a great lecture with no student involvement. My students remember very little of my good material.
always    usually    sometimes    seldom    never

3. I *approach* the extreme of having great student involvement with very little content communicated. My students remember almost everything of the very little that I teach them.
always    usually    sometimes    seldom    never

4. How do you respond to the following statement? Why?

"The alleged failure of the "open concept" to work in the public school is a good reason to avoid using it in Christian education."
*agree strongly     agree     disagree     disagree strongly*

5. Our total Sunday School time consists of _____ minutes. Generally, _____ minutes of that time are used to emphasize the content of the lesson to be taught. The remainder of the time . . . *(Complete the sentence.)*

*Note:* For additional help, please see "Lesson Plans and Planning for Learning" (see Appendix).

"Well, sorry we have to meet in the furnace room this morning, but you must admit, it's better than meeting in the stairway. And if you think it's hard to <u>listen</u> down here, you should have to <u>teach</u>! All your squirming around and all. . . ."

# 5

# Let Them Enjoy It! . . . and You

**Principle 5:** *Your teaching will be more effective if you develop a congenial environment to make learning more enjoyable.*

Escaping at the sound of the second bell in a cloud of dust, nine junior boys vacated their Sunday School classroom. As far as they were concerned, Sunday School had concluded at the first bell, or even earlier. But their teacher had detained them, intent on wringing a major point out of every tick of the clock.

This time the point wasn't even part of the lesson content. The point was "Sit quiet until the *second* bell."

That's all. In a surge of dedication the teacher reasoned that *someone* has to teach them to sit quietly in "God's House." After all, they will be expected to do so for the rest of their lives. What better time to learn than now, in the tender years of their youth?

A few doors down the hall another class meets.

Same age group, same church, and same curriculum materials. But a drastically different approach. The conclusion of the class hour finds this group of juniors reacting quite differently to the last bell.

A couple of kids hurriedly tape to the wall the last section of a hand-drawn mural. The completed mural contains a full review of the entire quarter's lessons.

Some girls finish copying the words of a song the class had written that morning. Not exactly a song, but words in rhyme, sung to a familiar tune.

"There was a king of Babylon
   his name was Belshazzar."

And there were other verses. Together they told the main points of the entire narrative. But the central concept was reinforced seven times—once each time the chorus was repeated.

The class had written:

"Kingdoms come and kingdoms go,
Kingdoms come and kingdoms go,
Kingdoms come and kingdoms go,
But God's Word is forever!"

The class had even chosen the tune to use. It was that grade school song, "B-I-N-G-O and Bingo Was His Name."

Which class enjoyed learning more? And which *learned* more?

If we were forced to choose between *enjoying* class and *learning* the Bible, we'd better vote Bible. But it's not either/or. The choices are not mutually exclusive. There are some observable principles which, if followed, will help cement the union of learning and enjoyment. Learning can be a joy!

## The Physical Environment Is Important

Many small churches have fascinating stories of how space problems were handled. It is the old problem of what to do with all the people you don't have classes for. We've heard of the church that has classes meeting in its choir loft, pastor's study, stairways, lobbies, and busses. Yes, busses!

These space problems are sometimes brought on by over-dividing, trying to have more classes than necessary. Sometimes they are the by-product of burgeoning growth, too rapid to be assimilated by the facilities. Often the problem is caused by severe budget limitations. Whatever the cause, few churches can long endure overcrowded conditions or inadequate facilities. Facilities either expand or attendance drops off.

One of the first churches I was associated with had mottos and quaint sayings adorning the cracked plaster walls.

One of them was:

"A class for every age, and a room for every class."

Or something like that. It was a goal that was never quite

attained even though classes were meeting in the office, kitchen, and a converted garage with a roaring space heater. The church was too small to afford a bus.

## Sardine-Style Learning Drives People Upstream

People soon weary of sardine-style learning experiences. It drives them upstream. They move on to more comfy quarters.

When the physical environment begins driving people away it's not just a building problem, it's a ministry problem—a teaching problem.

Even the best of content will not edify empty chairs. First-century Christians may have worshipped in the catacombs, but the boredom and sluggishness of Christians at the end of the 20th century may often stem, in part, from the inadequate physical environment of some of our churches.

Physical environment, social atmosphere, and personal relationships may be more closely interrelated with each other than some would imagine.

*Sometimes* the most beautiful and functional classrooms are the setting for minimal learning.

*Sometimes* very inadequate, overcrowded and uncomfortable quarters become the setting for great learning experiences.

But as a rule, every Sunday School should be interested in improving the physical environment of its classrooms in every way possible.

## Keep It Comfy and Attractive

Some problems are easier to locate than others. For example, heat, drafts, and stale air blow learning out the window. Fast.

But the causes of boredom, sleepiness, and sameness are a bit harder to identify. So after the heater and air conditioner are properly functioning (or better, before) we should turn attention to what we intend to accomplish in Sunday School. The room should be designed and equipped accordingly.

## Sit and Soak in the Sanctuary

Some people putter around the church with their mind in neutral, intent on tuning out all intellectual exercise. Call it meditation, or daydreaming, or sitting and soaking. It is the prelude to souring. Purposeful, thoughtful, worshipful reflection is often only a nod away from the sit-soak-snooze variety.

Dimly-lit sanctuaries with candelabra and stained glass may be uniquely appropriate for either reflective worship or an intellectual catnap. But the goals of the Sunday School class should include learning and the development of ministry-relationships. Both of these are very worshipful activities, but may be dampened in a cold, impersonal, church building with straight rows all facing front.

An "environmental creative alternative" to the quiet cathedral is in order.

## An Institute, Institution, or a Day Care Center

Sunday School often earns curious reputations by default.

It's a haven for little old ladies. Is it?

It's a modified child-care center with baby-sitting facilities for the care of adults. Is it?

For those who have the dream that Sunday School can be a Bible institute where learning is valued and seriously pursued, here's a word of encouragement: It can be! With a bit of planning and work.

Physical environment can work wonders toward this goal. If the sanctuary/auditorium is the only physical space available, plans should be made to improve lighting, and, if necessary, to provide a lapel mike for the teacher, and to make provision for audiovisual materials such as chalkboard, overhead projector, and screen.

Growing, learning Sunday Schools may progress in less than ideal situations. However, we should aim at making rooms as attractive as possible. Not necessarily as *expensive* as possible, but attractive. Draperies, carpeting, paneling, and a can of paint will contribute to a pleasant atmosphere. Clean up the stack of materials which has accumulated behind or on top of the piano. When compared with the result—a better place to learn—it's really not much work.

## Keep It Light, Open, Airy

In ages past, Sunday Schools thrived on little cubbyhole roomettes adjacent to the church's bigger rooms. In such situations, the church education program was often confined by those architectural limitations.

Confined in more ways than one. There were big rooms for opening exercises and little rooms for teaching.

Most growing Sundays Schools ran out of little rooms long ago and now seek alternatives. Interestingly, the solution some have turned to is a decided improvement in learning environment.

That solution, the so-called open concept, replaces the cubbyholes with light, open, airy, rooms—large rooms—for teaching. Several classes often meet in one larger room. It's not just a changing fad in Christian education. It is better for learning because it allows for involvement, activity, participation, and audiovisual media, all of which suffer in the cubbyhole. It is also far less expensive to construct than the traditional compartmentalized Sunday School building.

## Keep It Flexible

Since variety in teaching is important, a good classroom should lend itself to more than one seating arrangement.

Valid learning experiences can still happen in less-than-ideal classrooms, but we must strive for creativity in spite of our limitations. If we are strapped with fixed seating, we needn't add to the problem by being bolted to only one teaching method (see chapter 4).

Another thought: One shouldn't be too anxious to acquire the old pews for his class when the church buys new ones.

## Keep Audiovisuals in Mind

If there is one thing worse than sitting through a class where no visual aids are used, it is sitting through a class where visual aids are used but can't be seen.

Even older buildings can be well equipped with projection screens, electrical outlets, room-darkening drapes, chalkboards, bulletin boards, and projection stands.

The increased use of audiovisual media in secular education should say something to the Church!

## We Need a New Class but Where Will It Meet?

Many growing Sunday Schools are continually challenged by the need for more Sunday School rooms.

By that phrase, some people still mean the little cubbyhole roomettes that churches customarily provided next to those big rooms. A beautiful new educational building may be a future dream, but there's something that can be done now.

The larger, more attractive rooms in the church usually house placid adult classes, often with room to spare.

In turn, active children's classes may occupy the kitchens, broom closets, hallways, and in mild weather, there's always the busses!

It's not always possible to build new rooms. But a study by the church leaders or a Christian education committee may suggest some better alternatives.

A slight adjustment in departmental structure may allow the best rooms in the church to be used for the major educational goals of the Sunday School.

With the implementation of exciting audiovisual resources and a core of well-trained teachers, most Sunday Schools will find light, airy, attractively-decorated rooms ideal for larger numbers of pupils than could be accommodated in the old cubbyholes.

Current curriculum resources lend themselves with flexibility to larger classes with small group activities.

Current construction trends, including acoustical ceilings and carpeted floors, will allow for many people learning in small group situations throughout a larger room.

The open concept may actually combine the strongest benefits of both small and large groupings. Some activities, such as the presentation of a visualized lesson by a "master teacher," will be appropriate to the large room. Other activities associated with small groups can function very well in table groups or activity centers throughout that larger room.

In this way, the important element of the physical environment can significantly contribute to a good social atmosphere and deepening personal relationships.

## Practice While You Teach—13

Concept: *The physical environment is important.*

Use these points to evaluate the physical environment of your class.

1. Overcrowded conditions is (a) a problem that I have; (b) a problem that I have solved; (c) a problem that I would like to have.

I solved it (would solve it) by . . . *(Complete the sentence.)*

2. As I think about my classroom through the eyes of a visitor, I can make the following observations:

(a) Regarding attractiveness . . . *(Complete the sentence.)*

(b) Regarding comfort (including heating, cooling, lighting, seating) . . . *(Complete the sentence.)*

3. I could make my classroom more adequately equipped by:

    a.

    b.

    c.

4. Our current facilities could be used more effectively if . . . *(Complete the sentence.)*

5. *Complete this sentence with an idea that is attainable:*

The development of personal relationships in my class would be enhanced if the facilities were . . .

## The Social Atmosphere Is Crucial

I believe it was a shrewd old travel agent, with a twinkle in his eye, who originally said, "People like to go where people like to go."

And whenever a secretary, maintenance man, or window washer overheard him, they added, "It's true!"

And it is. It shouldn't bewilder us that "kids enjoy class where kids enjoy class."

It's true of adults too.

Part of the package deal called "congenial environment" *can* be learning. Though habits are hard to change and there is the extra charge of a little hard work, it's well worth the effort one has to put forth.

## The Promise Premise

Once while observing a first grade Sunday School class, I discovered a teacher who engineered her class by what might be called the *Promise Premise*. It went something like this.

"Last week some of you children made me very unhappy. Do you know why?"

No one was prepared to hazard a guess.

"It is because you were naughty. You were not quiet in class. Do you know why I want you to be quiet in class?"

Some probably had ideas, but wouldn't 'fess up.

"Is it because I want to be mean to you?"

Hmm. New thought.

"No. It is because I want you to sit still and be quiet so you can learn God's Word.

"Why do you come to Sunday School?"

"That's right. We come to Sunday School to learn about God."

Now, here comes the Promise Premise.

"How many of you want to learn about God?"

Unanimous.

"Then how many of you will promise to sit very quiet so we can learn?"

Again unanimous.

*The Promise:* "Be quiet so you can learn."

*The Premise:* "Kids learn best while being quiet."

It's too bad that promise will be forgotten in about as much time as it took to vote.

As for the premise, is it wrong to expect the attention of the class? Not necessarily. When something interesting is happening, all normal kids can, and will, tune in—even those livewire preachers' kids. Those who don't, P.K. or otherwise, should be lovingly corrected.

The problem with the Promise Premise—"Be quiet so you can learn"—is that kids *do not learn best* while giving abject, motionless, trancelike attention to lectures dispensed by adults.

The story of congenial environment, happy-place-to-be-learning, has a different plot and an exciting twist-ending: students enjoy learning!

## If Silence Is Golden It's Sometimes Tarnished
The silence is golden syndrome calls for attention in the young married department, too.

"I just can't get this class to take part," the teacher told me.

I made a mental note. Just a few weeks before, the pastor had complained that the young adults in his church wouldn't get involved.

So here's the tarnished-gold corollary:

*A:* For 15, 20, or more years we teach people to sit quietly in Sunday School and church so they can learn.

*B:* As they enter young adulthood, those same people go through "ministry-shock" as they are suddenly confronted with the happy news: "You are the gifted members of the Body of Christ. The purpose of the church is mutual edification. Now, who has something to share?"

If we value silence as gold in our *learning* situations, we will reap the disheartening result in general church life: people are too tarnished from inactivity to reflect biblical concepts of mutual ministry.

## High-F Openings and Why They Flunk
Sunday School was about to start. As was the habit, most of the adults were standing in the vestibule. It appeared that they were enjoying one another. It is good for believers to be together on the first day of the week.

The Sunday School superintendent was legitimately concerned. It is not good to start late. He mounted the platform and announced the opening song. The one destined to play the piano was now on the way to the instrument.

There was, it seems, a tinge of detectable resentment toward the people who were enjoying Sunday School out in the lobby. The ones who knew what they were there for began to sing them in.

"Really sing it out," they were told. "Let's bring in those latecomers."

That first verse of "Glad Day" progressed as well as might be expected under the circumstances, and without the aid of all those latecomers. But the chorus was the moment of truth with devastating consequences.

"Is it the crowwwnniiinnnngggg daaaayyy!"

Who is ready for a high "F" at 9:30 A.M.?

"All three verses now."

This was a good evangelical church. Sunday evenings were great. Sunday mornings, not bad. Congregational singing was a happy part of the services. But with 20 assorted sleeping souls scattered throughout the sanctuary, "high-F singing" was just too much. Or not enough.

Perhaps the folks in the lobby made the more enjoyable choice. But what will happen if one of them gets elected superintendent next time around?

### Remember the Travel Agent

One shouldn't be too critical of the unfortunate superintendents and teachers who are acting out the drama of traditional Sunday School week after week.

When we have opportunity to constructively effect change, it would be good to remember the words of the travel agent:

"People like to go where people like to go."

That may be our cue to tone down the singing. It is certainly valid to caution: Are we keeping it warm and alive? Are we fostering sharing-caring relationships in that Sunday School class? Are we constantly evaluating everything we do through the eyes of our prospective visitors? Do people feel welcome who do not already know the traditional evangelical ropes?

### "Welcome!"
### Want to Return? Or Crawl under the Rug?

For instance, a lot of what we do to welcome visitors may make them want to crawl under the rug. And that's difficult with wall-to-wall carpeting!

A brief fellowship time at the opening of Sunday School has helped many adult classes to make visitors feel at home. It also helps the regulars get better acquainted.

Most adults in church today are hungry for this kind of informal and friendly atmosphere so lacking in our church experiences. Careful attention to this crucial area of atmosphere is often the key to relationships that are vital.

## Practice While You Teach—14

Concept: *The social atmosphere is crucial.*

Use these points to evaluate the atmosphere in your Sunday School.

1. When it comes to Sunday School, I think that the average Christian is looking for . . . *(Complete the sentence.)*

2. *How do you respond to this statement? Why?*

"It is not right to expect any class, of any age-group, to learn in silence."

agree strongly    agree    disagree    disagree strongly

3. I help my students to feel like it is *their* class, not just *my* class by . . . *(Complete the sentence.)*

4. I allow time for informal "fellowship"—for visitors to be informally welcomed, for regular attenders to get better acquainted.

always    usually    sometimes    seldom    never

5. If a person came to my Sunday School class who was not a Christian, and did not have a church background we would . . . *(Complete the sentence.)*

## The Personal Relationships Are Vital

Ed Ross taught junior boys. Today he's in heaven, but there are boys scattered all over the world who remember him as their favorite teacher.

The Sunday School had a little rule: teachers shouldn't give presents to the kids. It was probably a good rule. One child in a family could be left out. Some teachers couldn't afford it. Things like that.

But World War II had just ended and junior boys only remembered wooden toys and empty toy shelves, due to war priorities. Then came the "Thimble-Drome Racer" craze. I think the racers were eight or ten dollars.

Ed wanted to do something special for the boys, but didn't want to make trouble at Sunday School. His solution? Ed owned a used car lot and service station. So he asked us, "How about you boys dropping by the station after school. You do some work for me, like cleaning windshields and sweeping up and I'll pay you with these neat racers we sell at the station."

I don't think our labor was worth much, but our whole class had "Thimble-Drome Racers."

I remember a trip to the mountains to play in the snow (this was Southern California). It was in a brand new '47 Pontiac station wagon with wooden sides. Being a dealer, he drove all the good ones.

Then there was my first time ever to see a professional baseball game. The Los Angeles Angels in the Pacific Coast League were playing. Los Angeles didn't have a major league team until years later.

Ed's classroom was always full. Several boys from unsaved families came, stuck around, and are now serving the Lord. Some of us from Christian homes were encouraged to enjoy Sunday School while others in the same church were being turned off.

But it wasn't just the trips and toys; Ed was our friend. Most people remember a teacher like that. I remember Ed Ross and was influenced by him in spite of the fact that he read his Sunday School lesson while sitting on the table in front of our cubbyhole classroom. I remember him because of the personal relationship. He was a friend.

## Training Plus

So the encouragement is appropriate: get all the training possible, become skillful with methods and resource materials, but above all be a friend.

I was a problem to some teachers. Hard to believe that the preacher's kid could carry on like that in Sunday School. But God used a teacher whose strongest quality was friendship to keep me turned on to Sunday School at a time when so many kids turned off.

Friendship is Christian. And the use of a modest segment of Sunday School time for building personal relationships through Christian fellowship is certainly consistent with the goal of increased Bible learning.

It is amazing the way discipline and boredom problems evaporate in the warmth of friendship. Teachers may need to spend a little time during the week in addition to that congenial class hour, but that's what discipleship is all about.

In fact, an impersonal *content-only* approach is inconsistent with the very fiber of Christian ministry. Astounding things happen to a teacher's effectiveness when his relationship to his students becomes a relationship of *ministry-influence.* That's something a teacher earns through involvement.

It's not just the teacher's responsibility to be a friend. He should foster an environment in which friendships between class members can grow.

Adults, teens, and children are hungry for personal relationships, informal settings, and personal involvement. Sunday School can make it happen.

## Sunday School Is for Body Building

Depersonalization, that sensation of being caught in the cogs of the machinery of society, drives people on a groping quest for belonging. "The Lonely Crowd," one writer called it.

Often sociologists speak of "primary" and "secondary" relationships: relationships close, relationships casual. As people find fewer and fewer primary relationships, the urge for acceptance and personal involvement intensifies.

We do not have to suggest apologetically that the Church is uniquely equipped to meet these needs. It will be equipped if we capitalize on personal relationships.

The Sunday School is ideally suited as a time and place. Capitalizing on personal relationships is not to be substituted for biblical content. Rather it becomes an opportunity to communicate and interact with biblical content. It becomes an opportunity to nurture ministry-relationships between believers. An opportunity to edify one another in the context of group Bible study and prayer.

Sunday School began as a time of special lay-involvement. It is unfortunate when the lecture-only pattern robs the body of the personal fellowship and relationship-building that can be a Sunday School class' specialty.

A 40-minute lecture and a party announcement is not enough. A more adequate provision for growth in Bible knowledge and Christian fellowship should include opportunity to share in ministry.

The benefits of Guided Discovery Learning go beyond learning itself. They often include actual involvement in mutual ministry.

## Amateur Hour

There's a need to climb out of the rut and reexamine our goals and priorities. If we started over from the ground up, it is doubtful that we would design a half-hour opening with the superintendent as emcee followed by dismissal to 20-minute class segments for learning.

Sunday School is at times the amateur hour of church ritual. As the Sunday School hour or its opening assembly takes on the contours of a formal church service it sacrifices the very thing it should specialize in: informal learning in an atmosphere of warmth and friendliness.

If an opening assembly time can contribute to the learning goal, and if it can be planned for interest and variety, it *may* serve a justifiable purpose in some situations.

However, no church can afford to waltz in the ruts while learning incentive and precious teaching time are buried together.

## A Total Hour

Sunday School should be an hour of participation in learning.

If the aim is Bible learning, and if we are consistent with that aim, we will tend to rearrange priorities away from traditional patterns.

In many places, Sunday School remains little more than a curious holdover from earlier days when it was provided as a sanctified babysitting service conducted simultaneously with the adult worship hour.

If we properly understand the obligation Sunday School has toward Bible learning we will view time differently. A full hour is not too long to devote to teaching objectives. That is especially true if our teaching objectives include group involvement.

Most current curriculum materials require at least one hour for full implementation. However, the most common objection is lack of time.

And where is the time going? One-half to three-fourths of the hour is frequently consumed on things not directly related to the learning objectives. It is a curious commentary on our stewardship, logic, and priorities when we spend the money to purchase Sunday School materials but refuse to spend the time to properly use the materials we buy.

## Discipleship Is the Goal

"It is my job to give out the Word. I can't help it if they don't like it."

The teacher was defensive about his failure to build warm relationships in his class.

Another man was overheard saying, "I don't really care how they feel about me; it is Christ I am pointing them to."

A third teacher excused his unwillingness to spend time with his students outside class by saying that he was not a youth worker.

"I'm just a Sunday School teacher."

Just? In their own way, each of these three expressed his disregard for a key concept in the ministry of Bible teaching. The imperative of the Great Commission is the discipling of people for Christ. That discipling is carried out, to use the words of Scripture, by "going," "baptizing," and "teaching." Facing the implications of that great command to the Church demands that we teach with discipleship in mind.

## Discipleship and Personal Relationships

Mark suggests something interesting about Jesus' ministry to His disciples. He called them for two purposes (Mark 3:14). The *second* purpose was "to send them out." The *first* purpose was that they "might be with Him."

It's a fine point, but a valid one: it is impossible to disciple people we do not spend time with.

Jesus walked with those disciples. He talked with them, He ate with them, He prayed with them, and He changed them by being with them.

As for us and our ministry, if content alone would do it, a set of tape recordings could replace the teacher. And it could be turned off at the *first* bell!

Spiritual growth toward discipleship operates on the wavelength of personal relationships. We have all noticed that people just do not respond well to teachers they do not like. And students do not learn very much from teachers who have alienated them.

The personality of the teacher is secondary to the authority of the Word (see chapter 2), but for benefit or for detriment, the personality is still important.

The life and influence of the teacher determines success or failure in discipleship far more than teaching technique does.

## Discipleship and Modeling

A teacher shouldn't expect a student to progress in Christian growth further than he is personally prepared to lead him. It is comforting to know that sometimes that does happen. But the general pattern remains today as Jesus described it years ago:

"Everyone, after he has been fully trained, will be like his teacher" (Luke 6:40).

That principle is another reason that teachers will be judged so strictly (James 3:1).

There really is no place for the attitude, "I don't care how they feel about me; it is Christ I am pointing them to." Rather, there is a sense in which a teacher ceases to be a discipler to a student when that student exceeds him in spiritual maturity. Paul invited people to copy him (1 Cor. 4:16; 11:1; Phil. 3:17; 4:9; 1 Thes. 1:6; 2 Thes. 3:9). It was a major emphasis of his ministry.

After we've done all we can to develop a congenial physical environment and a social atmosphere that makes Sunday School a happy place, we cannot escape the bottom line of responsibility.

Our success as a teacher will be determined by the style of relationships that we build. And to fulfill the commission to make disciples, we must consistently model the truth we teach.

## Practice While You Teach—15

Concept: *Personal relationships are vital.*

Use these points to evaluate your relationships with your students.

1. If I were starting from the ground up designing Sunday School, I would find it essential to include the following elements . . . *(Complete the sentence.)*

2. The students in my class that I have the most difficulty reaching are . . . *(Complete the sentence.)*

I could do a better job of establishing friendships with them if I . . . *(Complete the sentence.)*

3. My Sunday School class may never be a total answer for the need my students may feel for deep, intimate, personal relationships, but we could approach that objective if . . . *(Complete the sentence.)*

4. *How do you respond to this statement? Why?*

"It is wrong to pattern Sunday School after a traditional church service, since that would rob the class of the opportunity for participation and mutual ministry."

*agree strongly     agree     disagree     disagree strongly*

5. The thought of my students making me a model of biblical truth to copy, as Paul invited people to copy him, makes me feel . . . *(Complete the sentence.)*


Yes!

Yes! Sunday School teaching can be a more valid learning experience:

- if we will relate the Bible to the life-needs and experiences of the students.

- if we will involve the students in Scripture as authority.

- if we will direct our teaching toward specific, measurable learning aims.

- if we will reinforce the lesson with student participation in Guided Discovery Learning.

- if we will develop a congenial environment to make learning more enjoyable.

# Appendix

## Lesson Plans and Planning for Learning

1. Understanding the Lesson Plan
2. Focus: Techniques for Student Participation in the Approach to the Lesson
3. Discover: Techniques for Student Participation in the Exposition of the Lesson
4. Respond: Techniques for Student Participation in the Reinforcement of the Lesson
5. Audiovisual Involvement

### I. Understanding the Lesson Plan

There is a great deal of agreement that a well-planned Sunday School lessons has three parts. The variety of terminology can generally be narrowed down to three basic concepts:

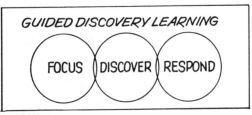

DIAGRAM 14

- *Focus* / Approach—"Grab them where they are!" You get pupils' attention, launch the lesson (various approaches include raising a question, probing a problem, giving background information).
- *Discover* / Exposition—"Take them where you're going!" Students hear and discuss what the Word of God says (narratives, doctrines, principles) and begin thinking of possible implications for their lives.

- *Respond* / Reinforcement—"Tell them where they've been!" Apply Bible truths to lives; help pupils make obedient responses to the Lord.

Assuming that the teacher has selected, or been assigned, good biblical content as the substance of the Sunday School lesson, here are some ideas. Perhaps he can help facilitate student participation in learning through that three-part lesson plan.

Active student participation in one or more divisions of the lesson plan should be our goal.

### II. Focus: Techniques for Student
### participation in the approach to the lesson
## Using an Agree/Disagree Opinion Poll as an Approach to Learning

*Description* A series of opinion statements on a pertinent subject are asked. Class members indicate whether they agree or disagree. Often a series of agree/disagree statements are duplicated on a sheet of paper so students can mark their opinions in written form.

Variations include only one agree/disagree statement (usually to introduce the main concept of the lesson), and expressing opinions by raising hands, standing, or changing positions in the classroom.

It is important to note that the statements used for agree/disagree discussion should not be so clearly correct or incorrect that individuals lose face for their answer. The best agree/disagree propositions are the kind that predictably would suggest two opinions. At the same time, they should be the kind of propositions that a clear focus on the lesson content would clarify.

*Examples of Agree/Disagree Statements*

[ ] Agree  [ ] Disagree  A teenager was told by his parents not to associate with another teen. When an opportunity to witness came up, he was justified in ignoring their wishes and spending time with the other teen.

[ ] Agree  [ ] Disagree  The Christian's goal is to convert the world.

[ ] Agree  [ ] Disagree  A good Christian would never under any circumstances partake of alcoholic beverages.

[ ] Agree  [ ] Disagree  A Christian passed a stalled car on a freeway ramp. Although he knew it was unlawful for him to stop, he was right in stopping to offer help.

[ ] Agree  [ ] Disagree  It is a sign of spiritual and emotional immaturity for a Christian to become angry.

*Values of Agree/Disagree*

1. This technique will readily capture the interest of a usually uninvolved class.

2. It is an excellent icebreaker to encourage open expression.

3. It provides a comparatively nonthreatening way to involve the timid. They will be intellectually involved through simply marking their worksheet or raising their hand if they choose not to enter into discussion defending their opinion.

4. It will stimulate *thinking*—a definite prerequisite to learning.

5. It will identify beliefs and values of the class so that the teacher can more realistically plan to meet needs.

6. It will demonstrate the need for God's revelation and clarify the class' commitment to scriptural principles rather than man's opinions.

## Using a Question as an Approach to Learning

*Description* The attention of the class is directed to a question or hypothetical situation as an initial effort of involvement in the content planned for the lesson.

*Examples*

*1. Question Response*  Use an overhead projector, poster, or chalkboard to graphically communicate a question. Ask for individual responses on 3″ x 5″ cards. The commitment of writing an answer is far more effective than simply asking the students to think of an answer. Have the students read the answer they have written; or collect cards and read them anonymously.

2. *Situation Response* Cartoon a situation and ask the class to respond to a question such as, "What is wrong here?" or "What Bible principle needs to be used here?"

3. *Circle Response* A question or controversial statement is tossed out for a short response by each member of the group as you move quickly around the class. Discourage lengthy responses since the idea is to solicit initial, nonthreatening responses from everybody.

4. *Neighbor Nudging* Each person is asked to discuss a given question with the person next to him for a given period of time. Usually two or three minutes is ample. This immediately gets the entire class involved and thinking about the subject matter you will be leading them to consider. This is one easy way to involve a large group where seating is fixed.

5. *Triads* The class is informally grouped by threes for discussion to be carried on in one of several ways. For instance, (a) all three can discuss together, pooling knowledge and experience; (b) all three can participate, asking persons one, two, and three to take a different aspect or viewpoint; (c) a role-play situation can be suggested in which the first person plays one assigned role and the second person offers some response. The third person reports the dialog to the larger group and critiques what persons one and two said.

## Using Play-Reading or Simple Dramatization as an Approach to Learning

*Description* In touching real life, a Bible lesson should focus on a problem to solve, a curiosity to satisfy, a frustration to relieve, or knowledge for life (see chapter 1). One of these can be readily translated into a simple play, with the parts read or enacted by members of the class.

*Examples*

1. For a lesson about Paul's courageous suffering for Christ, write a simple play showing unnamed Christians complaining, griping, and generally showing their need for just the principles that the lesson is intended to underscore.

2. A series about Bible prophecy and future events could be

introduced effectively with a dramatization of contemporary people discussing their frustrations or doubts about current events. This could close with a punch line like, "I really wish we knew more about what the Bible does teach about the future."

3. A simple play could show Abraham preparing to leave the city of his origin, leaving behind his great wealth and fame. As a friend argues with him about the foolishness of his decision, he affirms his faith in God, something so significant it is recorded in Hebrews chapter 11, centuries later.

4. A lesson about tactful and skillful witnessing is effectively introduced with a dramatization of a sincere but very ineffective witness who insults, stumbles, and generally offends the one he witnesses to. The use of theological terms and religious jargon leaves communication in a shambles. Most classes would be really interested in a principle-oriented exposition after being involved in watching the negative model.

5. Simple dramatizations of the characters in the "Good Samaritan" story, carefully translated into contemporary situations, could effectively create interest in what Jesus really taught about being a neighbor.

*Values of Play-Reading or Simple Dramatizations* The attention level of the class is at an all-time high when they are listening to the voices of their peers. We can "grab them where they are" by structuring a simple dramatization of the very kind of problem the Scripture lesson is intended to solve. It will not take long and with most groups it will require no rehearsal. But the concepts verbalized in the play will be remembered long after a lecture would be forgotten.

## Using Music as an Approach to Learning

*Description* A song is used to introduce a concept that becomes the focus of attention in the Bible lesson. This could be an inspirational song that provides the setting for the Bible lesson, or a song that focuses attention on a problem or frustration where the Bible can provide the answer.

Many popular songs are open-ended so far as providing an answer to the deepest hurts and frustrations that people are facing.

Such a song can form a ready point from which to demonstrate the practical relevance of a Bible lesson. Depending on the situation, it may be more appropriate to read words or phrases rather than play the recording.

Whether it is a problem song or an inspirational song, it is often desirable to divide the class into listening teams to note concepts to share in response to the song. This could also build a bridge to the lesson content while involving the class.

### III. Discover: Techniques for Student Participation in the Exposition of the Lesson
#### Using Guided Discussion in Discovery Learning

*Description* Discussion need not be a pooling of ignorance. Although there are ample examples of classroom discussion at its worst, discarding the technique on that account would be as foolish as eliminating preaching because we've heard poor sermons.

Guided Discussion in an effective learning tool because:

1. It is not a substitute for the teacher's careful preparation as discussion per se sometimes becomes.

2. The teacher remains in charge of the situation. Careful planning, timing, grouping, and moderating minimize the opportunity for one or two people to dominate or monopolize discussion time.

3. The discussion is directed toward achieving specific learning goals, not merely the airing of opinions.

4. The conclusions are not open-ended. The discussion is planned to facilitate the discovery of truth already revealed in the Bible.

5. The discussion is tied into the teacher's overall lesson plan and is used to support, not replace, teacher-directed learning.

*Examples*

*1. Buzz Groups* The class is divided into groups of four to six persons who are assigned a topic to discuss, based on a Scripture passage being analyzed. A specific time should be alloted. It is usually helpful for one person to serve as a reporter to write the group's conclusions to be shared with the larger group.

*2. Panel Discussions* When using panel discussions, the key is to assign (or otherwise provide) representatives to present insights or concepts based on Scripture. As this is done, different facets of the Bible lesson are brought out in a way that will command attention from participants and observers.

*3. Grouping by Content Outline*   In this situation, the subpoints of the Bible outline are assigned to different groups who are given directions for studying and reporting. As each group shares its discoveries, the overall outline of the lesson is completed. It is important that each group has specific instructions such as the following:

Divide the class into four study groups, assigning the following verses to each group for directed study.

*Group 1:* 1 Corinthians 3:5-9
*Group 2:* 1 Corinthians 3:10-14
*Group 3:* 1 Corinthians 3:15-17
*Group 4:* 1 Corinthians 3:18-23

Instructions: (1) Read the passage of Scripture. (2) Summarize what it teaches about the judgment seat of Christ, and/or the role of the minister. (3) Specifically, what does it say we should *not* do? What does it say we *should* do?

Allow 5 to 7 minutes for this discovery exercise. Instruct the groups to write down their discoveries. After they have a chance to study and record their discoveries, allow time for groups to share what they have found (two minutes per group).

*4. Grouping to Discover Biblical Answers to Questions*   Question response, situation response, circle response, neighbor nudging, and triads (techniques mentioned previously as *approaches to learning*), can also support *Bible Discovery* by assigning a particular passage of Scripture to each group for its investigation, study, and reporting.

*Values of Guided Discussions*

1. Guided discussions provide a comparatively easy way to allow many people to be involved within a short period of time.

2. When the conclusions or discoveries of student-peers are shared, interest and attention will be at a high level. Retention will increase proportionately.

3. Repetition of valid conclusions will reinforce learning. A

teacher could scarcely restate the same conclusion six times without running the risk of monotony. Six groups, reporting their own findings concerning the content of a Bible passage will not only hold interest, but will enhance the application of the Bible lesson.

4. Asking several groups to apply scriptural principles to contemporary situations will invariably enrich the practical application of the Bible lesson.

5. Members of the Body of Christ need the opportunity to edify and encourage one another as the Holy Spirit guides them into understanding. A carefully planned discussion situation can be a growing experience for believers.

6. We are all far more likely to remember and apply the things we discover and pass on to others than the things we are simply told.

## Using Research Projects in Discovery Learning

*Description* In order to gain more information on a given subject by means of direct involvement, individuals in the class are assigned or volunteer for research projects.

A problem or situation is presented to the class and the assignments are made on that basis. The class members then work on the research project and report their findings later in the class session or the following week.

*Examples*

*1. Time Lines and Charts* Individuals or groups can be involved making a time line, or charts, or lists of persons or events in which research is required. Projects could be listing the major events in a historical section of Scripture on a poster, or locating certain events on a time line or dispensational chart. This provides an opportunity to involve members of the class directly. They will be more eager to share material that they discover themselves.

*2. Reference study* Assignments can be made to gather information through the use of Bible dictionaries, Bible encyclopedias, commentaries, Bible atlases, concordances, topical Bibles and Bible versions or paraphrases. The assignment may take the form of listing different interpretations of a given passage, finding background information on the geography or culture of given land, or clarifying some historical point.

*3. Maps* Class members might be involved in making a map locating the major areas where certain biblical events took place. Maps made by those who are participating in the class will mean more and teach more than maps that the teachers find in a book.

*4. Team Teaching* The use of research projects may facilitate team teaching. Members of the class could be given the assignment of finding out certain information and preparing a report on that material to present to the class.

## Using Inductive Bible Study in Discovery Learning

*Description* The student studies the Bible directly for himself to discover (1) what the author was saying to the people to whom he wrote, (2) what he meant when he said those things, (3) what those things that he said mean to us today.

This method is particularly helpful in showing the student that he is directly accountable to what the Bible says for the decisions of his life.

A particular passage or topic can be assigned. Usually a passage of Scripture is better. It is the student's responsibility to dig out the meaning. He can use tools such as a concordance, Bible dictionary, and encyclopedia, maps, and books on Bible geography and customs. For this method of study, commentaries should not be used, however, since this is *the student's* study.

*Example* It is helpful to use four or five key questions to give direction to the student in his inductive study. The student should not be made to feel threatened if he comes up with a wrong conclusion. Misconceptions can be corrected in gentleness.

| *Question* | *Aids In* | *Applied to John 8:1-12* |
|---|---|---|
| What does it say? | Observation | An adulterous woman was brought to Jesus. Law said she was guilty of offense deserving capital punishment. He did not alter the Law. He did express mercy. Protected her without compromise. |

| What does it mean? | Interpretation | There's room for mercy in justice. Christ forgave the woman. Evident claim to Deity. *God* forgives. |
|---|---|---|
| What does it mean to me? | Application | Jesus is just as anxious to forgive me. And I should balance justice and mercy in my relationships with people. |
| What does the Bible say about this elsewhere? | Correlation | Fornication is considered sin (1 Cor. 6). God offers forgiveness in the midst of sin (Rom. 6). |

*An additional question:* How can I effectively communicate this concept to others? *(Communication)*

## IV. Respond: Techniques for student participation in the reinforcement of the lesson
### Using Creative Writing as a Reinforcement of Learning

*Description* Specific projects based upon Bible study not only make it more interesting, but greatly reinforce learning and retention. By providing an assignment that is based upon discovery of Bible knowledge, creative writing reinforces discovery learning.

As class members write about their thoughts, feelings, and beliefs, retention increases tremendously beyond that of simple hearing.

*Examples*

1. *Scripture Paraphrasing* Students respond positively to the project of paraphrasing Scripture, writing it in their own words. That simple task of rephrasing Scripture involves many of the steps that may constitute learning—reading with comprehension, rethinking, assimilation, verbalizing, writing, and rereading the finished product to others. Used in connection with other teacher-directed learning activities, the Scripture paraphrase is a great tool for reinforcing and applying Bible principles.

2. *Letter Writing* The variations are endless. Here are some suggestions:

(a) After studying the account of the feeding of the 5,000,

each class member writes a letter to a friend as if he were actually present at the Sea of Galilee, and wants others to know what he had seen of Christ's power.

(b) Students imagine that they were prisoners in the Philippian jail the night Paul and Silas were there and the jailor was converted. Write a letter to a close friend telling him or her your observations.

(c) The students write letters as if from Zaccheus to accompany the return of overpaid taxes. The letters should include a full explanation of why the money is being returned.

(d) Class members imagine that they were one of the young shepherds keeping sheep at Bethlehem on the night Jesus was born. They write a letter to a close friend to explain the exciting experience.

*3. Diary Writing*

(a) Students write a brief diary describing Nicodemus' nighttime encounter with Jesus.

(b) Students write a brief diary as if written by the Philippian jailor after the events of Acts 16:25-34.

(c) Students write a diary of the paralytic at the pool of Bethesda, including the day before his healing, the day of his healing, and the day after his healing.

*4. Tract Writing*

(a) After studying the message of Jonah at Nineveh, class members design and write a tract suitable for Jonah to use to help announce his message.

(b) Students write tracts for children, based on Luke 18:15-17.

(c) The class writes tracts for distribution in Chorazin and Bethsaida, according to Matthew 11:21.

*5. Song Writing* Writing words to fit a familiar tune.

(a) Children, youth, or adults can summarize any Bible story by setting it to rhyme and singing it to a familiar tune.

(b) Students in groups can be assigned different segments of an unfolding Bible narrative to set a familiar tune. Then all the groups come together to summarize the entire story set to music.

(c) Youth and adults can articulate their response to the

message of a given Bible lesson by writing new words to a hymn of praise, summarizing their own praise to God.

(d) The Psalmist David turned all kinds of experiences into psalms of praise to God. The content of a Sunday School lesson can be divided into separate concepts, with groups writing a psalm of praise to God based on the insights of the Sunday School lesson.

6. *Poem Writing* A teacher can encourage a "feeling" response to lesson content by assigning groups or individuals to write simple lines on subjects included in the lesson. Concepts like dedication, redemption, kindness, forgiveness, love, and so forth, make appropriate subject matter for poetry as a classroom project. Students who have studied poetry in school respond readily to free verse, which is based on meter rather than rhyme. Two common poetry forms are the *haiku* (17 syllables, in 3 lines— 5-7-5), and the *Tanka* (27 syllables in 5 lines—5-5-7-5-5).

## Using Simulation of News Media as a Reinforcement of Learning

*Description* Bible learning can be reinforced through preparing or observing presentations of newspaper story simulations, or simulations of TV or radio newscasts or interviews based on Bible content.

*Examples*

1. *Newspaper Story*

(a) In the biblical setting: Individuals or groups can research a Scripture passage and write it up in the form of a newspaper story. They should describe what took place following the formula questions, Who? What? When? Where? Why?

(b) In the contemporary setting: Using this approach, individuals or groups study a passage of Scripture with a view toward contemporary application of Bible principles. Then, translating the Bible story into contemporary settings, the students write up-to-date news stories illustrating the Bible principles.

Example: After establishing the application of the parable of the four soils to modern witnessing situations, groups in the class can write a simple newspaper account of a contemporary experience in planting the seed in each kind of soil. The class can identify which kind of soil is being presented in the modern situation.

*2. Roving Reporter Interview*   Individuals in the class study a passage of Scripture and put themselves in the place of a person in the Bible story. They are later interviewed regarding their responses and feelings.

Example: A roving reporter could interview the lame man who had just been healed by Jesus.

*3. Simulated Television Telecast*   Students can present their discoveries in a Bible story as if it were a telecast.

*4. Talk Show Interview*   The lesson material can be presented as a talk-show type interview with a Bible personality.

Example: Noah could be featured on "Meet the Press." Or a well-known television host could interview Moses after his experience of leading the Israelites out of Egypt.

*5. Man-on-the-Street Interview*   The entire class can study a passage of Scripture with a view toward putting themselves in the place of eyewitnesses. Following their study, a television-style man-on-the-street interview can be conducted to bring out every possible facet of the story.

Example: Class members become "participants" in the story of the feeding of the 5,000. Different groups study the four Gospel accounts. The reporter then conducts short interviews with the bystanders in an effort to uncover "what really happened here today."

## Using Role-Playing as a Reinforcement of Learning

*Description*   A problem is acted out with individuals identifying as much as possible with the characters. A discussion of the situation may follow or the role play may lead into the lesson theme.

*Examples*

1. Individuals in the class are asked to adopt the attitudes of characters in Bible stories and then adapt these same attitudes to present-day situations.

Examples: Ananias and Sapphira speaking on whether or not the church's mission budget should be raised. Or, Good Samaritan story characters in the role of local businessmen.

2. A person is described for whom many things have already gone wrong. Someone is assigned to play the role of this person reacting in a typical way to some unjust complaint from their husband or wife. The class is then confronted with the truth of Galatians 5:22 and a replay of the role is done based on the practice of that verse.

3. Role reversal is an interesting way to enter into the feelings of others.

Example: A situation can be suggested where adults assume the role of teens or vice versa when discussing some frustration of family or church life.

4. A child reacts like a very selfish person when asked to perform a duty of housekeeping. Then this behavior is compared with a biblical principle. The class replays the role in accordance with the Bible principle.

## Using Creative Art as a Reinforcement of Learning

*Description* The students prepare art projects to demonstrate a concept, their feelings about a concept, or certain facts discovered from Bible study.

As in other teaching methods, this encourages the student to *think* about how he feels or what he believes. The student is thus involved in learning.

Further, the student must grapple with his feelings, thoughts, and beliefs so that he may express them to others.

Creative art can take several different forms: drawing, lettering, commercial ads, collages, and various handcraft projects, photography, and so forth.

*Examples*

*1. Cartoons and Advertisements* The students can do cartoons or advertisements to illustrate characteristics of either a Spirit-led man or a carnally-minded man.

*2. Collage* A collage can be made communicating man's spiritual need and Christ as the answer; or various facets of biblical truth.

*3. Photography* In groups of three or four, students can pantomime a Bible story and photograph it with a Polaroid camera. The pictures can be arranged on poster board and captioned, or identified by other students in the class.

*4. Doodling* Students can doodle a picture of how they would have felt if they were with the disciples when Jesus stilled the storm, or some other event. Artistic talent is not required. Students can share their feelings and why they drew what they did.

*5. Lettering* Students can letter titles for parables or biblical statements which illustrate the content of the parables or statements.

*6. Design* Students can make designs to illustrate biblical concepts or stories.

*7. Mobiles* Creative art can be used as a method of discovery learning. For instance, students can make mobiles in which each part of the mobile pictures some facet of biblical truth which they must dig out of the Bible for themselves.

Examples: The fruit of the Spirit; major facts in Moses' life; missionary trips of Paul; events in the last week of Christ's life.

*8. Posters* Students can make posters to communicate major facts from a passage of Scripture; or certain characteristics of a person who is obedient, or not obedient, to certain principles of Scripture.

### V. Audiovisual Involvement

In addition to students being involved in the learning process through the use of Bible learning activities, students can be involved through the use of audiovisual media.

The same formula applies: greater involvement means more learning.

A lot of helpful things from a lot of helpful people have been said about audiovisuals. Some of the principles commonly agreed on are included in the following paragraphs.

Audiovisual materials are probably most *effectively* used with youth and adults. They are most *commonly* used with children.

Why? It's true that teachers tend to feel insecure with new methods and materials, but audiovisuals for children have been around a while.

Perhaps some teachers just do not realize what audiovisuals can do for the learning of their students.

A big complaint is lack of preparation time. What can be said? When students—children, youth, or adults—learn, it is worth the time.

It makes sense. Audiovisuals communicate through the eye-gate, not just the ear-gate. And for just about everybody, audiovisuals make learning more interesting, more enjoyable. Concepts that are abstract become more understandable.

It is worth the time.

### Visualize What You Verbalize!

1. In preparing audiovisual materials, the teacher should begin with a good, easy-to-follow outline of the lesson material to be covered. This will provide a foundation to work from in preparing all of the visual materials.

2. The teacher can use maps to locate places which he makes reference to in the course of the presentation of the lesson.

3. Charts and diagrams visualize concepts (such as dispensations) in a more understandable way.

4. Visuals can be prepared from key statements and thought-provoking questions which the teacher wishes to emphasize. Seeing as well as hearing will more than double the impression that is made.

5. Visuals may be prepared to depict situations or statements with which the teacher wishes his students to particularly identify. This can be done by using cartoons, slides, filmstrips, overhead transparencies, and, most effectively, films.

6. When wishing to emphasize the significance of a different translation or paraphrase, it may be visualized by putting it on a flip chart, chalk board, or overhead projector.

7. The forte of audiovisual media is in its ability to motivate. When possible use audiovisual materials to drive home a life application. This can be done with extreme effectiveness through the use of short discussion films.

## For Further Reading . . .
## VICTOR BOOKS for Christian Education Leaders